sign language interpreting:
a basic resource book

REVISED EDITION

Sharon Neumann Solow

Illustrations by
Frank Allen Paul

A Publication of Linstok Press
Burtonsville, Maryland

LINSTOK PRESS

Published by Linstok Press
4020 Blackburn Lane
Burtonsville, MD 20866
Printed in the United States of America
ISBN 0-932130-22-4

19. 95

Acknowledgments

I wish to express my gratitude to Virginia Hughes; she "taught me everything I know."

My first boss, mentor, replacement and good friend, Norm Tully, without whom I might have become a psychologist. I also wish to express my gratitude to the National Center on Deaf people for the tremendous support and assistance rendered by its personnel in the preparation of the first version of this book. And to my first teachers, Lou Fant, Virginia Hughes, Audree & Ken Norton, Eric Malzkuhn, Ralph Neesam, Agnes Foret, and so many more.

I wish to also thank Arlene Benson for her wonderful assistance in editing the first manuscript, Barbara Dreyfus who helped me to develop the concept of this book, John Kralick for his endeavors in compiling the first bibliography, the National Association of the Deaf and especially Mel Carter, Jr., for all of their assistance and belief in the original publication and for publishing my first book. Thanks to Marina McIntire for her fine editing of the first version of this book. My gratitude to Don Renzulli for always being willing to lend his creative hand to this and many other projects. To Verden Ness and Barbara Olmert and the folks at SMI for all their help in the revision, and for pushing me to do it, my thanks.

I feel deeply the gifts my students have given me along the road of this career. They have taught me much more than I have taught them. Thank you all. That is also true for my wonderful colleagues who have given me so much to think about, so many great conversations and have raised this field to its present heights. My thanks to MJ Bienvenu who has graciously agreed to write the foreword of this revision and who has contributed greatly to my thinking and to the profession. And to Lou Fant for his shaping and encouragement of my thoughts in this field and for his contribution to this book go my sincere thanks.

My deepest gratitude goes to my parents, Don and Hertha Neumann who gave me the language and the desire to enter this field. And now to Barbara, who has given Dad a second chance at life. Further I thank the Deaf Communities in which I grew up and the ones I have been involved with all my life. They provided me with so much information, motivation, reinforcement and experience.

Finally, I thank my family. Sheila Hall, my sister, for the collegial and personal support. Larry Solow for his assistance in clarifying my thinking and for his support both personally and professionally. Megan and Jered for their patience and encouragement, and for being such great kids, allowing me, with such grace and generosity, to be a Mom and a professional.

Foreword

It has been 20 years since the first draft of this book was being finalized and sent to the publisher. In those 20 years, the field and the world have changed in some dramatic ways. Many principles still stand, but much is quite different than it was in the '80's. It was like a walk down memory lane to realize some of the shifts in perspective obvious in the original version.

In an effort to be timely and useful, I have finally undertaken the revision of this book, and the product of that labor sits in your hands. If you are a Sign Language interpreter that metaphor suits you because your product sits in your hands. Like this one, I hope yours will continue to grow with the profession and with you as an individual. I look forward to learning together and doing another serious revision in the future with your input.

It is my hope and desire to be helpful through the writing of this book and its revision. Your input may already have found its way into these pages, because this book is a result of the many people I have had the joy of working with throughout the world. I still welcome your input. Please communicate your ideas and suggestions to me at SNSBEAR@aol.com or through Sign Media, Inc., 4020 Blackburn Lane Burtonsville, MD 20866.

Sharon Neumann Solow

The field of interpreter training is beginning to come of age. It may be true that we cannot teacher signers to be interpreters, but it is certainly true that many signers can learn to be interpreters. Ms. Neumann Solow has written a book that will facilitate learning the art of Sign Language interpreting. For the student it presents the important issues and expertise which must be mastered. For the teacher it presents an excellently arranged guide. Interpreter training has suffered for lack of adequate materials. This book will help end that dearth, and stimulate our work to greater success.

Louie J. Fant, Jr.

Interpreting is an interesting field of work. It is also a difficult profession—it involves language, culture, cross-cultural communication, interpersonal skills, and often an understanding of oneself. It takes a lifetime to become a master interpreter and when you think you are getting there, you find new information that needs to be learned—not only about the profession, but the languages used within the profession. English has been recognized as a language for at least 800 years, but ASL was given recognition only about 40 years ago. The study of ASL is still evolving and everyday we learn something new that may have been overlooked for many years. Americans study English from the day they begin school until the day they graduate. It has only been since the late 1970's that ASL (not Sign Language) classes have been offered. Numerous students enroll in ASL programs, but only a few strive to become interpreters. While it is true that some interpreters have never gone to an ASL class, like those with Deaf parents and those who have associations with D/deaf people, all of them need special training in interpreting to become professionals.

Sign Language Interpreting: A Basic Resource Book, the Revised Edition by Sharon Neumann Solow demonstrates the basic concepts of interpreting. It is written in such a clear, easy-to-understand style that anyone who wants to know more about interpreting and what it involves will gain from reading it. It discusses areas that interpreters most often encounter when working and it serves as a useful tool in assisting students of interpretation to understand the profession. This book provides a good introduction and a warm welcome for those who are interested in the field of interpreting.

MJ Bienvenu, MA

MJ Bievenu is a certified RID Deaf Interpreter, a Deaf Interpreter Educator, as well as an ASL Instructor for over 20 years.

Table of Contents

Introduction

The room settles, the speaker finds her position, clears her throat and begins. A few seconds later, a pair of hands reaches up and begins to form sentences in the air. These hands belong to an interpreter, who is taking the thoughts, words, emotions, and nuances of the speaker and putting them into a visual form of communication.

The second speaker finds his position. He is a leader in his community and begins his lecture. This man stretches out his hands and begins. A few seconds later a voice is heard. This voice belongs to an interpreter, who is transmitting the thoughts, words, emotions and nuances of the signer into an auditory form.

The Sign Language interpreter acts as a communication link between people. An analogy is in the use of a telephone— the telephone is a link between two people that does not exert a personal influence on either. It does, however, influence the ease of communication and the speed of that process. If the interpreter can strive to maintain that parallel positive function without losing vital human attributes, then the interpreter renders a professional service.

Throughout the day, every situation involving communication holds potential for the use of a Sign Language interpreter. Many activities that hearing people in the United States take for granted might be a source of great effort for a non-hearing person. Take, for example, telephone calls. One option for D/deaf[1] and hard of hearing people is the use of a telecommunications device for the D/deaf (TTY or TDD). Another is Visual Relay Interpreting (VRI) in which the interpreter is on camera and interprets for the telephone call at distance.

Casual daily encounters with people are often marked by deceptively simple communication that is often taken for granted. In a store, think of the ease with which communication occurs between hearing persons. One automatically and without effort says, "excuse me" on the street when bumping into people. When one's back is turned, it is normal to hear a friend calling out and to then be able to respond. A hearing person, without even trying, can tune in to a nearby conversation, a radio or television program or bit of news or one side of a telephone conversation, sometimes not even remembering where that little tidbit of information was picked up. All of these and more are examples of a world that is differently accessible for D/deaf people and non-deaf people.

The challenge for Sign Language interpreters is the equalization of communication for hearing and D/deaf people. Interaction between hearing and D/deaf individuals may present particular challenges because there are other things to consider beyond mere language differences. While it is often true that these people do not share the same language, it may also be the case that these individuals do not share the same culture. As interpreters, we must function in a very real way as the ears of one person and the eyes of the other. We serve as cultural bridges as well.

The situation of the Sign Language interpreter is unique in many ways. When two hearing persons from different countries try to communicate, both parties involved can hear. The foreign language interpreter is not required to pass on auditory information so much as to translate the words and inflections of speakers. By contrast, a Sign Language interpreter serves as a complete auditory link to the D/deaf person, who relies on the interpreter to know, for example, that an accent is causing misunderstandings, or that a falling branch has caused the others in the room to look out the window.

As first-class citizenship becomes more and more of a reality for all people, increasing attention is being given to the special ways in which we can offer everyone an equal opportunity to participate in the events of the world. The new catchwords are "equal access," including equal access to information. Interpreters can play an important role in this process of equalization by making information and people accessible. In order to live up to this challenge, we must strive to develop the necessary skills to best provide this access to the populations that rely on us to transmit information between them.

The skills required of a Sign Language interpreter start, naturally, with language competency. Interpreters must be fluent in both languages they use. In our case the two languages are English and American Sign Language, or whatever sign system is being used. (Different systems of manual communication will be discussed in depth in Chapter 2.) Beyond language capability, the interpreter needs some other sometimes subtle skills. As mentioned earlier, the task is not only transmitting from one language to another (with all the complexities of two different cultures), but also involves the inclusion of peripheral sounds and other modifications that apply to communication when a D/deaf person is involved and the complications arising out of working between two populations that often are of different power and status.

Our profession is relatively new and operates with little external regulation. Therefore judgment on the part of the interpreter is essential to one's functioning and vital to the development of the profession. That judgment must be a form of self-regulation for the interpreter and for the entire field, which in turn will influence the behavior and underlying attitudes of Sign Language interpreters. The basis for judgment must be reliable information and a solid philosophical foundation. A fundamental goal of this book is to provide some of that information for people new to the field and those who seek a higher level of sophistication in the area of Sign Language interpreting.

Definition of Terms

As in any specialized area of endeavor, Sign Language interpreting has its unique vocabulary.

A. Interpreting

1. Interpreting

The process of transmitting information from one language into another for the purpose of communication. Therefore, our work involves the process of transmitting English into ASL and ASL into English, typically for communication between D/deaf and hearing people. We traditionally view our work as occurring between D/deaf and hearing individuals, and that is the usual scenario. However there are occasions in which interpreters work an environment that has only D/deaf people or in a situation involving only hearing individuals.[2]

2. Transliterating

The process of transmitting spoken English into any one of several English-related or English-oriented varieties of manual communication and signed English into spoken English for communication between D/deaf and hearing people. Again, we traditionally view our work as occurring between D/deaf and hearing individuals, and that is the usual scenario. However there are occasions in which interpreters work in an environment that has only D/deaf people or in a situation involving only hearing individuals.

In this book the term "interpreting" is often used generically to refer to interpreting and transliterating, as defined above. Transliterating will mean specifically staying within one language. Notice the crucial distinction between transliterating and interpreting; only the latter involves the use of two separate languages. (See Chapter 2.)

3. ASL-English Interpreting

The process of transmitting meaning from ASL into English and English into ASL.

4. Gestural Interpretation

The process of transmitting meaning from a language (such as English or ASL) into gesture and gesture into a language form.

5. Sign-to-Spoken Transliteration

The process of transmitting gestured communication or English related or English-oriented varieties of manual communication into spoken English, typically for communication between hearing and D/deaf people.

6. English-to-ASL Interpreting

The process of transmitting spoken English into American Sign Language.

7. Spoken-to-Sign Transliteration

The process of transmitting spoken English into English-related or English-oriented varieties of manual communication.

Once again, Spoken-to-Sign "Interpreting" and Sign-to-Spoken "Interpreting" are the generic terms applied to transliteration as well as interpretation unless otherwise noted.[3]

B. Visual Communication

1. American Sign Language[4]

The language of the Deaf Community. It is a language in and of itself with its own grammar, vocabulary and rules of discourse. Also known as ASL, the Sign Language of D/deaf people or Sign Language.

2. Contact Variety

A variety of manual communication in which characteristics of both English and ASL are combined. Also referred to as Siglish, Sign English, manual English, or Signed English.

3. Manual Alphabet

The process of repeating the letters of the English alphabet on the hand. It directly represents the English spelling system. Also known as Fingerspelling or Dactylology.

4. Manual Communication

The generic term for any communication using signs and/or fingerspelling. This is also known as signing or signs.

5. Pantomime

A nonverbal form of communication which is not bound to a certain group of people who speak the same language. It is the freer gestural system of communication which crosses the boundaries of language. Pantomime is the way many D/deaf people get across some of the ideas they are trying to share when they are communicating with non-signing people or with foreign individuals. This will be discussed in depth in Chapters 2 and 8.

6. Minimal Language Competency

Used to refer to those individuals with little or no education, and whose command of ASL, English or any other language is either chronically poor or nonexistent. Also known as MLC, Minimal Language Skills, MLS, Minimal Communication Skills. or, MCS. (See Chapter 8.)

The Field of Interpreting

Interpreting is a challenging field with some unique qualities that set it apart as a profession. It would be difficult to find another field that offers such a variety of experiences. Interpreters serve in nearly every kind of classroom, professional, medical or legal setting, service situation, or therapy setting that occurs, and this list could be expanded indefinitely. To put it simply, an interpreter can be exposed to whole worlds of information and thrust into situations demanding professional preparation or training.

Historically, the interpreter was a person who worked with D/deaf people in some other capacity or who just happened to know Sign Language. There was no such thing as a professional interpreter. These people were the pioneers of the field as we know it today. Most of them volunteered, served with no expectation of payment, and, through their generosity, helped train the next generation of interpreters. Now things have changed to the point that interpreters are hired in many situations and are paid for their services quite consistently. No longer must D/deaf people feel obligated to a kind person who donated hours of personal time to help. Now a D/deaf person can expect, without excessive gratitude, a professional to handle the situation and to handle it well.

The evolution of our profession has been characterized by stages which reflect the societal and professional norms and attitudes of the times. Prior to the professionalization of interpretation, interpreters were volunteers and helpers, treating D/deaf people as needy and perhaps "less than" hearing people. A sharp reaction to that was the machine model in which the interpreter is likened to a telephone, adding nothing to the experience of D/deaf people and leaving nothing out. In an effort to more appropriately meet the needs of D/deaf individuals and human beings in general, the communication facilitator model came about where the motto was "meet the need". The bilingual-bicultural model aimed to take into account the variance in culture and language between D/deaf and hearing people. Other views of the approach we take as interpreters include the role of advocate for D/deaf people's rights, ally, arbiter between power groups and a model in which we admit to and function around the concept that we are not invisible, we are very much a part of the situation we function in and must respond to the work with those things in mind. Each model or approach was a response to the circumstances surrounding the D/deaf and interpreting community at the time and each is still in evidence in working interpreters in the U.S. and elsewhere.

In the latter half of the 20th century, there was a dramatic shift in the circumstances surrounding training for people who wished to become Sign Language interpreters. There simply was no training whatsoever, nor recognition of interpreters as paid or in any way professional as late as 1963. Now there are interpreter training programs throughout North America and Scandinavia, much of Europe, and many other countries. More and more information about Sign Language interpreting and the interrelationship of the experiences of the D/deaf and hearing people is being shared and taught. This growth can only bode well for the D/deaf and hearing people served by the interpreting profession. Interpreting service can be obtained from professionals who are prepared to render this service in a variety of ways.

[1]The use of "D/deaf" includes those Deaf people who have a cultural identity within the Deaf Community as well as those people who cannot hear and are not members of the Deaf Community.

[2] TRANSLATING: Translating, in common usage, is usually considered equivalent to the term Interpreting; however, it is specifically used in reference to the written task, with more preparation time.

[3] ASL-to-English interpreting and Sign-to-Spoken transliterating were historically called "reverse interpreting" and later, "Sign-to-voice interpreting." These terms are on longer in favor among professionals, but as in any are, terminology takes time to change.

[4] Hereafter referred to as ASL.

Chapter 1

Interpreter Role and Behavior

The Function of an Interpreter

The service an interpreter provides can be summed up as follows: interpreters attempt to equalize a communication-related situation so that the D/deaf and hearing participants involved have access to much the same input and output or can take advantage of the same resources. At base, interpreters are wholly involved with meaning. There is more to an interpreter's job than merely transmitting the signed equivalents of words that are heard or the spoken equivalents of signed utterances. Our function and goal is to take meaning in one language and fully express that meaning accurately in the second language. Because determining equivalence between expressions in two languages is extremely complex, interpretation is, by definition, extremely complex. An excellent discussion of the process of interpretation can be found in <u>Interpretation: a Sociolinguistic Model</u> by Dennis Cokely. After even a quick overview, it is impossible to think of interpretation as a simple task.

Confusion lies in the false sense that just by knowing two or more languages a person can interpret between them. Although fluency is certainly a prerequisite, there is a great deal more to

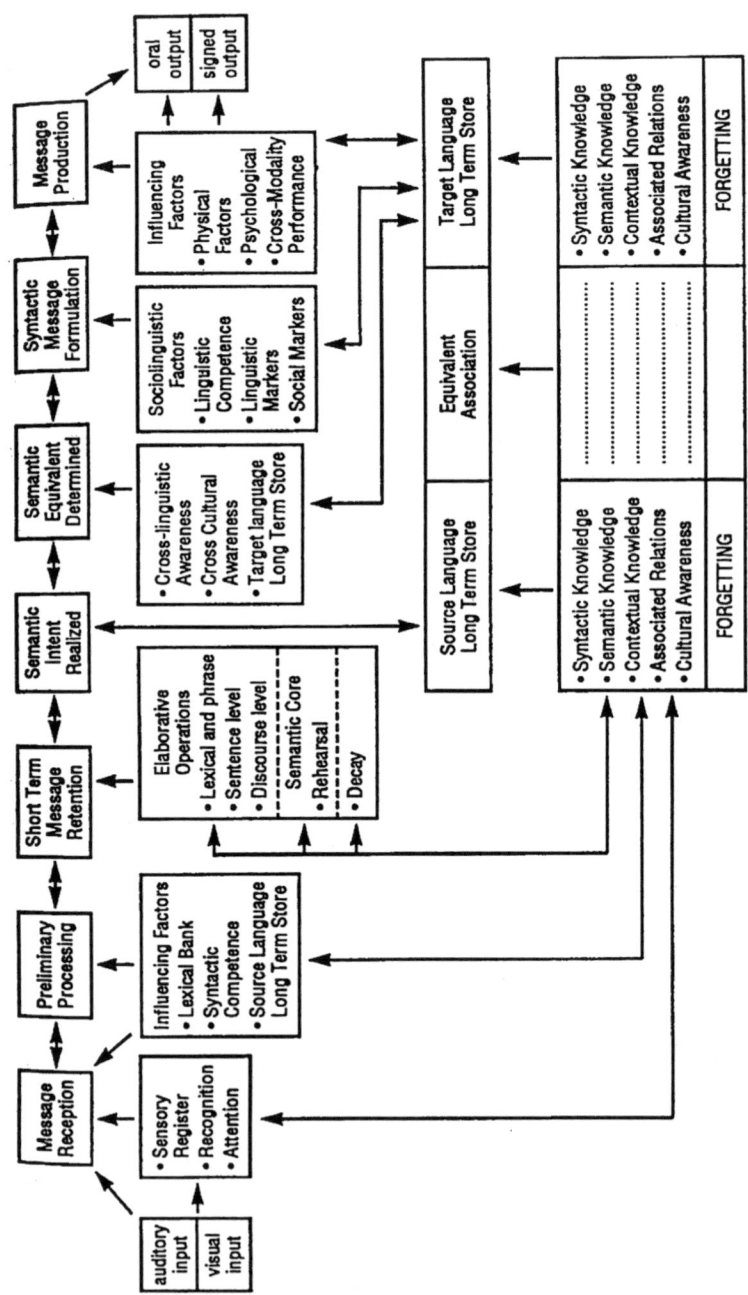

SOCIOLINGUISTICALLY-SENSITIVE PROCESS MODEL

interpretation than language skills alone. In the following chapters we will explore the skills, knowledge and attitudes required of an interpreter, and many of the situations they face.

Sign Language interpreting can be done consecutively or simultaneously. Outside of lectures, and other forms of relatively one-way communication, much of what we do is consecutive or quasi-consecutive. Simultaneous interpretation is the approach used in the U.N. and often in media where the interpreter is producing the interpretation at the same time the originator of the message is producing the message with little time between reception of the source message and onset of the production of the interpretation. Consecutive interpretation is much more natural than simultaneous. The source text is produced, the interpreter then transmits the interpreted version and the process continues. In a typical interview, say between a client and an estate planner, the question is asked, the interpreter then produces the question in the second language. The answer is given, the interpreter produces the answer in the language of the estate planner and so forth.

There has been a strong emphasis in our field on interpreting simultaneously. Wherever possible, consecutive or, at least quasi-consecutive, interpretation provides a much more productive and accurate communicative environment. It allows time for syntactic, semantic and cultural accommodation and therefore more natural language output.

Deaf interpreters add a resource to the field that is rich and extremely valuable. They may serve in any setting that a hearing interpreter might be utilized and can provide an incredibly important service in any number of settings. Wherever an interpreter is required, there is a likelihood that a Deaf interpreter would be productively involved. They are found at conferences, including international meetings, in more private settings, such as a doctor's office and everywhere in between. Typically, Deaf interpreters bring an extra level of cultural awareness and comfort to the task and can communicate more naturally and effectively with D/deaf clients under a variety of circumstances. The situation is generally a team set up. A hearing interpreter acts as the interpreter between the hearing clients(s) and the Deaf interpreter. The Deaf interpreter interprets between the D/deaf clients(s) and the hearing interpreter. This allows a more consecutive-like approach in solving difficult interpreting challenges. It is important that the two interpreters meet ahead of time to arrange the situation to their comfort and for efficiency.

Qualities of an Interpreter

The characteristics of a professional interpreter are many, and after a while the list begins to look like the Girl Scout Code or the Golden Rule. Interpreter behavior refers to actions while interpreting; however, there is no attempt to reform those who enter the field to become better or different people. Interpreters have a right to their individuality, but there are many qualities that can help to clarify the role and functioning of a professional Sign Language interpreter.

1. Flexibility

Interpreting requires flexibility. Interpreters are constantly bombarded with vocabulary and must be flexible enough to incorporate what is learned into their own usage. Flexibility is necessary in order for an interpreter to fit into any situation. Since interpreters are the vehicles for communication between many kinds of people, they should be prepared to fit into the various situations in which they find themselves. Interpreters conceivably can be used in any situation, from the most intimate to a huge public forum, from quite informal to highly formal settings.

Interpreters have worked in situations ranging from athletic events to zoology classes. Interpreters have been used at religious ceremonies that are new to them and very different from those of their own religion. Interpreters have responded to strictly oral situations, such as the interpreter who was asked to lipread to reconstruct the soundtrack of a film, the script of which had been lost, and there are interpreters who never rely on the oral mode. Sometimes an interpreter transmits from one silent mode into another while another interpreter then passes on the information to the hearing members of the group. In this instance there are two interpreters and only one who speaks.

Interpreters have even been used to help researchers understand the signs used by chimpanzees. During a single day an interpreter may be asked to interpret for a sports event and then for a very formal awards banquet. In that same day one consumer may prefer to use ASL while the next consumer will rely heavily on lipreading, and a third consumer may request a great deal of fingerspelling in addition to signs. Flexibility will help the interpreter fit into these different situations.

2. Objectivity

Objectivity is an essential quality of a professional interpreter. This quality requires showing no favoritism and not revealing one's own feelings while interpreting. The interpreter typically cares deeply about the welfare of the individuals being served, but must maintain a form of "detached involvement," caring about the people involved without investing personal feelings in the situation. If the interpreter becomes involved in an interpreting situation, it is quite possible that it could influence the interpretation; this in turn could affect the situation. By remembering the basic principle of the interpreter as facilitator only, it is possible to be more objective so as to do an effective job.

3. Self-discipline

Self-discipline is a quality that probably is the basis for most of the more specific items mentioned. Because interpreters work basically alone, with little or no supervision, interpreting is not an easy profession to monitor. It is nearly impossible to supervise the work of an interpreter. Often the parties involved are either signers who are D/deaf or speakers who are hearing, and typically the reason the interpreter is present at all is that there is no one else present who has bimodal skills. Therefore, neither communicator in such a situation is in an appropriate position to evaluate the effectiveness and honesty of the interpreter. It is thus the responsibility of the interpreter to set limits. The interpreter cannot be the sort of person who waits for others to enforce the rules, but rather must have an intrinsic set of values.

There is a joke that shows the power of the interpreter clearly. A D/deaf man stole a million dollars and buried it under a tree. After a long search he was jailed, but the money never found. The detective questioned him in jail with the assistance of an interpreter. The detective so frightened the D/deaf man that he finally explained in detail the whereabouts of the money. The interpreter said, "You can ask all you like, but I will never tell you where the money is!" Then the interpreter went and dug up the money! This joke takes the principle into the absurd, but the point is nonetheless significant that the interpreter must be of high integrity in order to be privy to the many things we are exposed to in the course of our work.

Self-discipline evidences itself in the interpreter who turns down an interpreting task that is not appropriate for that interpreter to handle. It is also Self-discipline that helps the interpreter to stifle emotional reactions and thus avoid influencing the people involved in the situation. Interjecting one's own feelings into a particular setting would be truly stepping out of the role of an interpreter; yet without Self-discipline, it would be quite difficult to prevent certain strong emotions from showing.

Behavior of an Interpreter

The actions of interpreters reflect on each other as well as on the interpreting profession as a whole. An attitude of professionalism is a characteristic that every profession needs in order to maintain the kind of standards that go along with being a professional. Self-policing is one function of the profession, as most professionals operate with little or no real supervision. As professionals, we are responsible for our personal growth as well as for the growth of our profession.

1. Fluency

In any target language, competence, spoken and signed, is necessary, along with the ability to "meet the need" by being fluent in whatever is required so that the most appropriate system can be used for each occasion. This necessitates an ability to assess the communication needs of the individuals relying on the interpreter for service. We often focus our efforts on building our sign skills and vocabulary; however, it is also essential to build our spoken vocabulary and skills. It cannot be overly stressed that an interpreter needs skill in both languages—not just one—in order to function properly.

2. Sensitivity

The interpreter needs to be sensitive to a unique position, the third and often unwanted party. "Unwanted" means that very often consumers of interpreter services must allow a stranger to know some very intimate details of their lives, and this must sometimes be difficult, even with the knowledge that the information will go no further.

It is difficult enough for a person to share private information with a person such as a social worker, doctor or lawyer, who by virtue of the profession is privileged to know. Think how much more uncomfortable it must be to have to reveal this information in front of a third person, no matter how vital that person might be to the process.

3. Tact

The interpreter must strive at all times to maintain a low profile, so as to avoid becoming the focus of the attention of the participants. Notice that there are times when this can be taken to unnecessary extremes, as for example, the time that an interpreter almost passed out from an allergic reaction to cigarette smoke rather than interrupt the class she was interpreting to ask a man to put out his cigarette.

On one occasion, an interpreter was in a mental hospital interpreting in a group therapy session. Across the room was a D/deaf person, and the interpreter was seated in the circle of people. One patient next to the interpreter kept asking why her hands were shaking. The therapist said all the right things, that the interpreter's hands were not shaking, that rather she was signing. But the patient could not seem to comprehend this and kept on mumbling to the interpreter that it would be all right, not to worry, and that lots of people are frightened at first in a mental hospital. Finally he held the hands of the interpreter, trying to "calm" her. These are unusual situations and require tact and careful handling.

4. Punctuality and Responsibility

Punctuality and responsibility cannot be stressed too much. It is essential to the entire experience that the interpreter arrive on time so the communication, which the interpreter provides, can proceed. Obviously, the interpreter is only useful while on the job, and absence removes the D/deaf and hearing person's bridge for communication.

On the other hand, it is important to remember that one problem that plagues many service professions is the misconception that the provider of the service can never be absent. This simply cannot be true. Human beings, as a matter of course, will have physical, mental, emotional or social reasons which will not allow them to be present at any and all occasions where they are needed. However, it is crucial to arrange either for a substitute interpreter or a change of date or time. An ill or inattentive interpreter would probably put in a less-than-effective appearance. This might be worse than an absence, since hampered performance could cause misunderstanding.

5. Self-awareness

The Sign Language interpreter acts as a link between individuals. Again, the analogy is in the use of a telephone as a link between two people that does not exert a personal influence on either. The interpreter strives for a parallel positive function without losing one's humanity. If this is maintained, the interpreter-client relationship will be on much firmer ground.

It is important to keep in mind that the satisfaction derived from an interpreter's work should stem from a sense of a communication job well done and not necessarily the repercussions to the client at some other level. To illustrate this point, an educational interpreter could consider the student's final grade a direct evaluation of one's skill as an interpreter. That interpreter would, in effect, be taking any credit or blame away from the participants in the class, the teacher and the student. Other problems that might result from this attitude might be a great deal of patronizing behavior toward the D/deaf student, checking on progress, and other displays of concern over the student's performance in the class.

There is also the possibility of a false sense of success or failure in the interpreter. It is conceivable that an excellent interpreter might interpret for a failing student, and a minimally skilled interpreter could interpret for a highly successful student. This is a point that might help us remember where our influence lies. We must value our skills in the area of seeing the client's needs and doing our best to meet those needs in the communications sphere, such as picking the appropriate sign system, finding a beautifully equivalent phrase for a highly difficult and heavily culturally laden piece of text, arranging the physical setting well and establishing a comfortable, non-threatening atmosphere.

6. Judgment

Perhaps another label for this quality is Common Sense, that not-so-common attribute we seek and admire as a guiding principle in our lives and the lives of others. This ability to determine the best course of action in any situation is essential to the functioning of an interpreter because we so often can influence situations so significantly. What we choose to do at any one time can slightly shift or even completely change the outcome of an event.

One area of judgment that I find interesting has to do with decisions about what we transmit and do not transmit. While Sign Language interpreters generally pass on the vocalized English equivalents of signed information, it is also necessary that they transmit significant auditory input into visual form. Actions and incidents may be puzzling to a D/deaf person unless environmental clues are transmitted by the interpreter. It may be that the reason that everyone in class turned their heads may have been because someone in the back of the room was coughing, or because a jet flying overhead had cut off the sound of the voices in the room. An interpreter explaining that a speaker has a very strong accent, that a clock is ticking very loudly, that the others in the room are very silent, and so on is "tuning in" the D/deaf person to various environmental clues. For example, a class was intently working on a difficult mathematical theorem when it suddenly began to rain. All the hearing students turned their heads to look out the window. The interpreter pointed out that the rain had begun falling so suddenly and loudly that it had startled everyone. The D/deaf student was surprised to learn that rain could make noise, and was able to understand such comments as, "Oh, I've no umbrella!" Though pointing out environmental sounds may be desirable, it would be impossible to transmit everything we physically hear, such as the regular ticking of the clock, or the sound of the wind or an occasional cough in the room. The interpreter must determine the relevance of a certain bit of auditory input within a given situation and then quickly decide whether or not to transmit that bit of information. The interpreter will, with extremely rare exception, faithfully transmit information presented by a speaker. However, sometimes there is simply not enough time to transmit all extraneous information, such as the accent or the lisp of a peer, or the sound of cars passing. This kind of information will necessarily take a back seat to the main information being transmitted.

We will constantly find ourselves returning to the term, judgment. Sooner or later, most professionals realize that their own sense of what is appropriate may be relied upon fairly heavily throughout their careers. This is also true of the Sign Language interpreter. Since we work with people and not things, there will always be intangible factors with which to deal. Interpreters make minute and huge decisions of this type and many others throughout their task.

Thought Questions

1. What is the basic function of an interpreter?
2. List five qualities of a good interpreter and discuss their impor-

tance. Give examples where they might affect a situation.

3. What are some appropriate bases for a sense of success or failure as an interpreter?

4. How could the interpreter transmit the concept of a constant clicking in the radiator?

5. Under what circumstances might the interpreter decide to transmit that information? Under what conditions might the interpreter decide not to transmit it?

Chapter 2

Sign Systems and Situation Assessment

Sign Systems

Sign Language is a generic term for many forms of manual communication. Many systems of signed English have been developed in response to a desire on the part of some educators who saw a need for a method to teach English to D/deaf children. Many of these English sign systems currently in use are the center of a great deal of controversy from linguistic and educational standpoints. As interpreters, we need not concentrate on the controversy at this point; however, for our own use and understanding, it is important to know the terminology and to remain current with the state of affairs.

There are two languages among the various systems outlined on the chart in this section *(p. 16)*. These two languages are English and ASL. All others are *systems of communication;* some are naturally occurring and some are contrived; most are based on both of the languages.

13

Terms

ASL

American Sign Language, the language typically used among D/deaf adults in the U.S.A. and Canada. A language in and of itself, with its own grammar, vocabulary and rules of discourse.[1]

Contact Variety

The generic term for naturally occurring varieties which incorporate traditional ASL signs, some newer and contrived signs, and fingerspelling in flexible grammatical order. Popular nomenclature for Contact Variety includes Sign English, Signed English, Siglish, and CASE.

Conceptually Accurate Signed English (CASE): The communication style characterized by the incorporation of traditional ASL signs, some newer signs, some contrived signs and fingerspelling, along with speech and speechreading, signed generally in English grammatical order in an effort to represent English visually. Signs are organized in English order with minimal changes, and English is usually mouthed as spoken in the original English that is interpreted, or English source text. Signs are used with an attempt to retain the meaning from ASL rather than English, so that "right" would be signed different ways depending on its meaning.

Manually Coded English

The generic term for contrived systems for encoding English in manual form. These systems of visual English are attempts to precisely teach the English language, both its grammar and vocabulary, through the means of speech and speech reading, and the use of a combination of traditional signs, newer signs, and contrived signs. Contrived signs are generally based historically on ASL signs. Signs are usually selected on a "one sign - one word" basis, deviating in some significant ways from the meaning of the original ASL signs. Sound and spelling are generally the deciding factors in sign selection, rather than meaning. Thus, all meanings of the word "right" would be signed the same, while "write" would be signed differently. Signs are placed in English order with signs to represent English grammatical forms, such as suffixes and prefixes. MCE was devised as a means of teaching English to youngsters. Sometimes referred to as SE, S-E or SEE systems, examples of MCE are SEE_1[2], SEE_2[3], LOVE[4], Manual English[5], and Signed English[6].

Rochester Method

The communication systems utilizing fingerspelling, speech and speechreading in an effort to represent English manually.

Cued Speech

A system of organized gestures used to aid in lip-reading. These gestures are used to distinguish between sounds that look alike on the lips, such as /b/, /p/, and /m/.[7]

Oral Method

The communication system that incorporates speech and speechreading only; no signs or gestures are involved in the oral method. This refers also to an educational philosophy emphasizing the exclusive use of speech and speechreading.

English

The language spoken, written and read by the majority of people in the United States, England and a number of other countries of the world.

Reader's Theater

A technique for presenting poetry, prose and plays using a certain amount of dramatic technique such as pantomime.

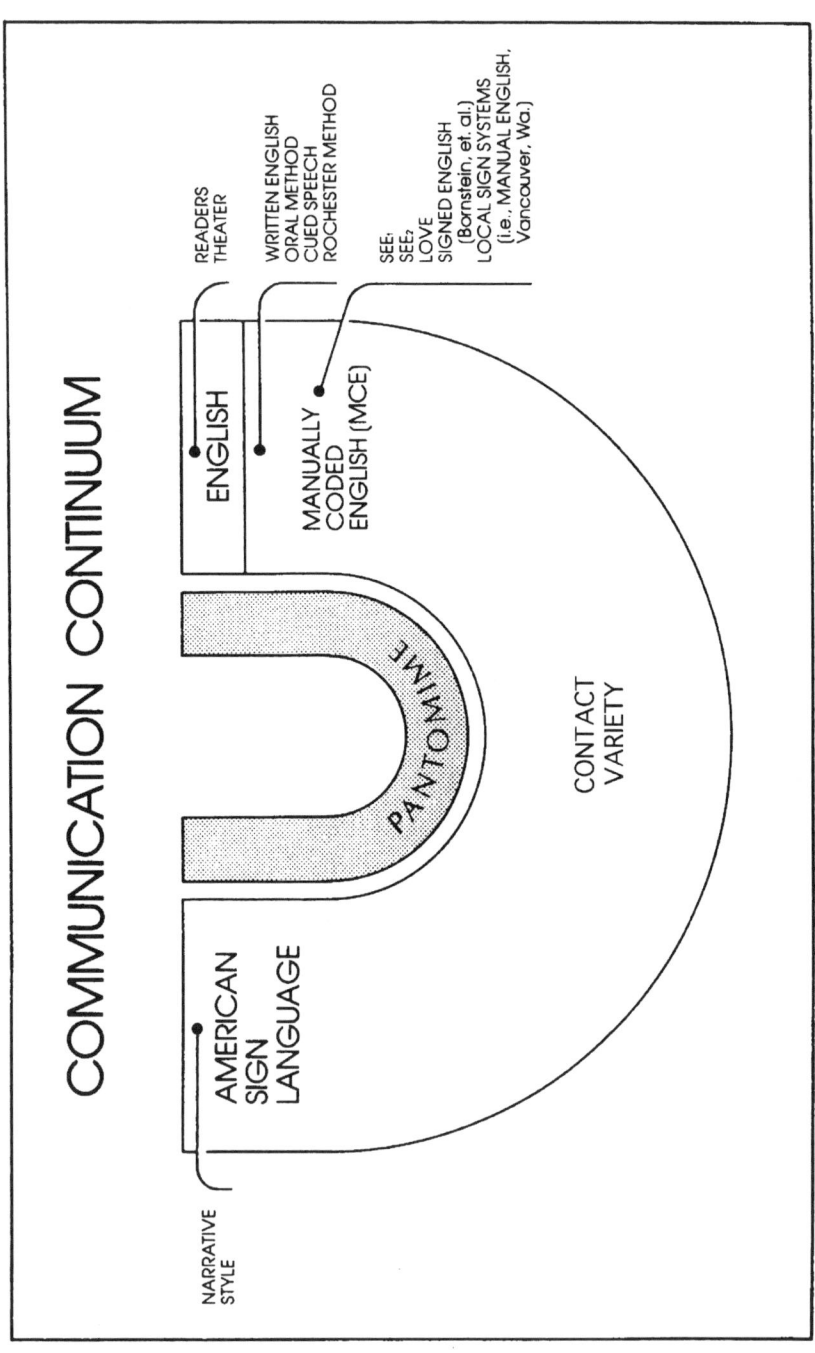

Pantomime

A more universal method of communication through gestures; a nonverbal system of communication. Communication through gesticulation, occasionally for one-to-one communication, often used in theater.

Narrative Style

A form of storytelling style, often incorporating techniques from pantomime in telling stories for theatrical effect.

Pantomime is included in the sign systems chart because it can play a part in the communication modes of and with D/deaf people. First of all, pantomime is the sole communication mode used by a small number of D/deaf people, such as those with minimal language competency (see Chapter 8). It is also a mode many D/deaf individuals may use with people who do not know how to sign.

As interpreters, we should be aware of pantomime so that we can incorporate pantomime techniques to make our communication—both our signing and our reading of signing—more effective and clear. We can borrow from pantomime to include such things as strategies for communication with individuals with minimal language competency. Pantomime, however, is not Sign Language and Sign Language is not pantomime. Many people make the error of confusing the two, perhaps because they are both visual; however, one is a language and the other is a means of communication, not a language.

Manually Coded English (MCE) is often referred to as the SEE systems after SEE_1 and SEE_2. These are sign systems that have been contrived for educational purposes. SEE_1, SEE_2 and LOVE all started out as a single system, but because of differences in approach, branched out into three separate systems. They still share many characteristics and basic tenets.

Although many of the signs are based on the traditional signs from ASL, these signs are not used in the same grammatical, syntactic or semantic sense as in ASL. For example, there are at least three signs in ASL which denote the various meanings of the English word "right," while a single sign represents this word in Manually Coded English.

Many of the systems on the chart are attempts to make English visible on the hands and/or mouth. Most of the visualized English systems were designed for use in the education of D/deaf children. As interpreters, we must remember that our task is not the improvement of D/deaf people's language (ASL or English), but rather the facilitation of communication between individuals. Sometimes a particular program will require the use of English or one of the systems of visualized English. In these cases, the interpreter basically contracts to transmit into and from that specified system upon acceptance of the position.

Situation Assessment

There are a number of assumptions that the Sign Language interpreter can make in determining the mode of communication to use with each D/deaf audience approached. Every audience will require certain modifications in style, vocabulary and sign system to meet its unique needs. The skill of the interpreter rests in part on the ability to make appropriate decisions regarding these choices. Probably the best and easiest way to determine the appropriate sign system is to ask the D/deaf persons in the audience themselves or to ask the organizers if they are aware of the D/deaf members' preferences as a whole. A danger here is that one cannot assume that all people, even those heavily involved with D/deaf people, are fully aware of the different sign systems and communication styles used among D/deaf people. Labels for these communication choices are not always shared or accurately used and the situation is further complicated by the fact that sometimes decisions are politically or socially influenced. Therefore, the decision is complex and it is often up to the interpreter to make this determination, based, of course, upon observation and interaction with the clients.

It is important to remember that any suggestions on choice of approach to communication discussed in this section are based on assumptions and that every individual situation will have to be weighed for appropriate service.

For most mixed and/or large audiences, such as mass media viewers, or people attending religious services or a public forum, the interpreter would most probably lean toward ASL as the primary mode of communication, since the largest number of D/deaf persons would be served by that choice. Again, it is important to check with the people in the audience, if at all feasible, in order to learn their own preference as to sign system. It is well to be aware that some D/deaf people are highly offended by the assumption of what they will prefer, ASL or English. There are political and social pressures that come to bear. This is likely a result of years of oppression of the Deaf Community, propaganda that ASL is somehow lower in status than English, that it is "bad language" or "poor English". Strong reaction to that oppression might be another influencing factor. It is also influenced by the availability of appropriately skilled interpreters or lack of same. Where the audience is mixed, invariably there is the need for more than one form of service. Often a transliteration is provided on one side of the stage and interpretation is provided on the other. There is no real compromise, although for years we have called Manually Coded English the compromise or middle ground within a mixed audience, it is still a choice with its own set of repercussions. Therefore the arrangements for at least interpretation and transliteration is essential to the communication needs in that environment. There may be need for different forms of transliteration rather than just one as well.

Many high schools and other educational institutions hire interpreters with the specific requirement that they use a particular style or system of MCE or Manually Coded English. The use of one of these specified systems would then be typically considered part of the contract or policy of the hiring institution.

Pantomime of a sort, in combination with some rudimentary and simple signing, is used for communication with D/deaf individuals with minimal language competency. This area of interpreting requires some very special and sophisticated skills. Interpreting for D/deaf people with minimal language competency requires time to stop and check for understanding, and time to get continuous feedback. The ability to both use and understand pantomimic communication is essential in this mode of communication. For those further interested in this area of interpreting, minimum language competency interpreting will be discussed at greater length in a later chapter.

Perhaps the most effective way to determine what service is to be provided, besides asking the clients involved which system they prefer, is observing conversation among D/deaf clients before the interpreting assignment, or conversing with the client(s), to determine the sign system that seems most comfortable for them. Such a decision carries a certain liability in that the clients might see the interpreter in the light of a primary interactor rather than a communication bridge that is not directly involved. It is also possible that an unsophisticated client might try to talk through the upcoming situation with the interpreter, which again places the interpreter in the role of a primary interactor. This kind of conversation should be avoided. With careful handling, the interpreter can maintain a comfortable level of involvement with the clients. It is helpful to simply explain the role of the interpreter if there is any confusion or inappropriateness.

Finally, there is another way to determine the best system to use while interpreting—the technique of reading one's audience. This means reading the body language and other nonverbal cues for evidence of comfort and/or discomfort with the signing system being used. If a confused or blank expression appears at the incorporation of certain signs, possibly those signs are unfamiliar. If there is a great deal of conversation about certain signs the interpreter is using, perhaps this is a cue that those particular signs or the system from which they derive is unfamiliar. If, on the other hand, D/deaf clients are constantly asking for the fingerspelled word for signs when initially presented, it may be an indication that they are more English-oriented and might prefer a MCE version of the presentation or that the skill level of the interpreter may not be adequate for the assignment. This back channel communication is an essential aspect of the feedback that guides interpreters throughout their work.

It is almost always preferable to ask the D/deaf clients directly involved what their choice of systems might be. If they are not available before the interpreting situation begins, or if they are not able to answer the question due to a lack of sophistication or experience with interpreters, then it is often helpful to check with others who have been involved with the particular situation, such as a previous interpreter or a professional involved. Previous interpreters are usually a very reliable source. Often, however, situations arise in which the interpreter can get little or no reliable information about the communication methods to be used. In such instances, it is appropriate to rely on the audience's response to the particular vocabulary and communication system chosen, with constant modification as the need arises or becomes evident, including incorporation of signs used by the D/deaf people in that setting.

Thought Questions

1. What is the function or basic reason for the development of many of the signed English systems?
2. How many true languages are involved in our sign systems? Name them.
3. What system of communication on the systems chart is 'universal'?
4. What system of communication is probably called for in interpreting a television program?
5. How is pantomime used in verbal communication?
6. How is the determination made as to how to sign certain vocabulary items in SEE_1, SEE_2, and LOVE?
7. What is probably the best way to determine which sign system to use in a given situation? Why?
8. What can the interpreter do while interpreting to assess and meet the communication need within a given situation?

[1]Baker,Charlotte; and Padden, Carol. (1978). <u>American Sign Language: A Look at Its History, Structure and Community</u>. Silver Spring, MD: T.J. Publishers.

Klima, Edward; and Bellugi, Ursula. (1979). <u>The Signs of Language</u>. Cambridge, MA: Harvard University Press.

Stokoe, William C.; Croneberg, Carl G.; Casterline, Dorothy C. (1976). <u>A Dictionary of American Sign Language on Linguistic Principles</u>. Burtonsville, MD: Linstok Press.

[2]Anthony, David. (1971) <u>Seeing Essential English</u>. Greely, CO: University of Northern Colorado.

[3]Gustason, Gerilee; Pfetzing, Donna; and Zawolkow, Esther. (1975). <u>Signing Exact English</u>. Alameda, CA: Modern Signs Press.

[4]Wampler, Dennis. (1971). <u>Linguistics of Visual English</u>. Santa Road, CA: Booklets.

[5]Gustason, Gerilee; Pfetzing, Donna; and Zawolkow, Esther. (1975). <u>Signing Exact English</u>. Alameda, CA: Modern Signs Press.

[6]Bornstein, Harry. (1983). <u>A Comprehensive Signed English Dictionary</u>. Washington, D.C.: Gallaudet University Press.

[7]Cornett, R. Orin. (1978). <u>Cued Speech and 'Total Communication'</u>. Washington, D.C.: Model Secondary School for the Deaf.

 Chapter 3

Physical Factors

D/deaf consumers must be able to see and be seen clearly and hearing consumers must be able to hear and be heard clearly. As interpreters, we need to prepare for and arrange the setting with this in mind.

Since eyes are controlled by muscles and ears are not, receiving communication through the eyes can be more tiring than through the ears. It is important that the interpreter remember this in planning the physical arrangements.

Position

The interpreter should be close enough to the speaker to make it possible for the D/deaf consumer to see both the interpreter and the speaker without turning or stretching whenever possible. At the same time, the interpreter needs to be sensitive to the speaker's sense of space and comfort. Some people feel uncomfortable with the interpreter too near or too far. It is also important to be near enough to the D/deaf audience so that they are not straining to see. The judgment of the interpreter is essential in determining the physical setup.

Being near the speaker can also aid the interpreter in hearing the speaker more accurately. Since the interpreter cannot look at the speaker directly, proximity is very important. The interpreter cannot rely on lipreading to help distinguish certain sounds, or on gestures that will aid in understanding. If a public address system is being used, it is important that the interpreters are situated in a position in front of the sound system speakers or that special speakers be positioned facing each of the interpreter stations. Otherwise the sound may be distorted or inaudible.

A decision must be made in each situation as to whether the interpreter should sit or stand. Logistics, use of visuals, and the number of D/deaf people in the audience should be taken into consideration. If there is a large number, it is usually best to stand for the sake of visibility. It is also best to stand during a platform interpreting assignment, or if the audience is any distance from the interpreter. When the speaker moves around a great deal, standing leaves the interpreter in a better position for quick and easy movement. The same is likely to apply if there are visuals being used.

If the presenter is signing, the ASL-to-English interpreter should be seated in front of the signer. If a microphone is needed, it should be placed where the ASL-to-English interpreter is seated. Since the interpreter is usually facing away from the listeners, the need for a microphone is greater than if all presentations were given from the front, facing the audience. If there are D/deaf and hearing people presenting as well as in the audience, then it is wise to have at least two interpreter stations. One interpreter position is on the platform while the other is in the audience facing the platform. The responsibility of the interpreters on the platform is to sign the spoken presentation and perhaps to vocalize signed comments and questions from the audience. The interpreters in the audience position have the responsibility of interpreting the signed presentations and sometimes signing to D/deaf presenters on stage who may be unable to see the platform interpreter. Such a situation may call for several interpreters to meet the needs. The circumstances are in actuality much more complex. Anytime an interpreter is involved in such a situation, flexibility, sensitivity and timing will assist the interpreters in providing thorough service. (See Chapter 7, PLATFORM INTERPRETING.)

Many situations call for different positioning. In a class-room, interpreters generally sit in front of the class, to the side and slightly forward of the teacher. In one-to-one situations, the interpreter and the hearing and D/deaf consumers generally sit in a triangular formation with the interpreter facing the D/deaf consumer, but quite close to the hearing party. Around a table or in a circle, the interpreter usually sits across from the D/deaf person(s). In court, the interpreter must be very careful about placement. There are rules of sight line for the judge, jury and attorneys. Interpreters must be audible when interpreting the D/deaf person's utterances to hearing attorneys, judges, members of the jury, and, importantly, to the court recorder. At other times interpreters will assist in "whispering" between client and lawyer. Naturally, the interpreter must be, at all times, visible to the D/deaf individual(s) relying on the interpretation.

Seated or standing, the interpreter needs to be located in a position where all the D/deaf people involved are able to see the interpretation clearly and where all the hearing people are able to hear any interpretation. In most cases it is advisable to have more than one interpreter station for a large audience of D/deaf people because it can be difficult to read signs from a distance. The problem of reading fingerspelling and lips at a distance is especially great. Video projection screens and/or multiple video monitors can bring the interpretation to visible field for large audiences as well.

There may be situations in which some D/deaf persons prefer the interpreter not to be in front of the room. For whatever reason, this preference should be respected. If this is the case, it is certainly the right of the D/deaf person to make the decision on positioning, as long as there is agreement among all the D/deaf consumers involved and as long as the hearing consumers' needs are appropriately met. Obviously, this requires the understanding that the interpreter may not be in the ideal position to hear what is happening in the classroom or lecture hall.

Positioning is a factor over which we generally have some control. Physical factors influence accuracy, accessibility and comfort of all involved. Try to find a position before starting the interpreting task so that time and information are not lost while you are trying to get situated. Note interpreter positions in the following illustrations.

1. INTERVIEW

2. CLASSROOM — TEAM TERP

3. PLATFORM — TEAM TERP

4. COURTROOM

5. SIGN-TO-VOICE (without microphone)

6. SIGN-TO-VOICE (with microphone)

7. TEAM INTERPRETERS

8. AROUND A TABLE

9. IN A CIRCLE

10. LARGE AUDIENCE (several interpreters in various positions)

Turn-taking and Teaming

If the situation is long or strenuous, one interpreter will not be sufficient to serve the situation. It may be necessary to have a number of interpreters to spell one another, either by time or by speaker. Interpreters in this situation take 15 to 30-minute turns. Others are assigned to speakers even if the presentation is shorter than 15 minutes so that the transition is smoother; they simply move to the front at the same time as the speaker. A reasonable guideline comes from research which shows that reliability of the interpretation reduces dramatically after 20 to 30 minutes of interpreting. It is important to note that when surveyed, interpreters were not typically aware of the reduction in their effectiveness after 20 to 30 minutes that was evident to the researchers, therefore the interpreter is not a reliable judge of maximum effective length of interpretation turns.

Spelling one another should be as smooth and as least distracting as possible. We work to avoid losing information in the transition so that those relying on the interpretation continue to follow the speaker throughout. The interpreter in front continues interpreting while the relief interpreter shifts into position. It is easiest and most effective to time the transition for a break in the discourse. If such an ideal break does not occur within a reasonable period of time, then the relief interpreter transitions in during a lower level break or pause. The transition should be relatively speedy and as little attention paid to the transition as possible. The focus must remain on the text that is being interpreted. The relief interpreter must watch and listen to prepare to interpret next. The primary interpreter determines the actual moment of the shift. The relief interpreter picks up the interpretation wherever the primary interpreter leaves off. Now the relief interpreter is the primary interpreter and the cycle continues.

It is essential that the relief or back-up interpreter has visual contact with the primary interpreter. The team needs to be able to see one another for a number of reasons. Eye contact provides the primary interpreter with feedback and back-up, it allows for both interpreters to be aware of one another's lexical choices, for the relief interpreter to be aware of any needs or problems that might arise. Teaming allows us to be more effective interpreters, to solve problems more easily when they arise, to learn from one another and to mentor one another.

Sound

The importance of interpreters being able to hear and to be heard cannot be over emphasized. Without the input or output of our work, the quality of the work is inconsequential. Some considerations in this area have been mentioned earlier. Proximity to the speaker or to the technological sound source is essential. Use of a microphone is highly recommended for any large group situation. The interpreter should arrive a bit early and, if necessary, rearrange the room for optimal sound and visibility. Auditory augmentation may be needed in the form of a hearing aid. There are hearing aids for those who just want to raise the volume or to make up for less than optimal hearing. There are mobile microphone and listener sets which look like little transistor radios or tape recorders and which the interpreter can place appropriately. This is used often in courtroom situations where it is difficult to rearrange the seating. The interpreter places the microphone wherever it will pick up the speaking best in the room and then carries the listener for improved audition under difficult circumstances. Technology has many solutions for us. Don't be shy about asking and arranging for optimal auditory arrangements.

Background

The background against which an interpreter works is a very important factor that relates to visibility and ease in watching for the D/deaf person. Background pertains both to the interpreter's clothing and to the background behind the interpreter. Your clothing should offer a plain, solid color that contrasts with your skin. Interpreters are often highly visible and must attend to personal style and hygiene very responsibly, while always remembering that their hands and faces must be clearly visible to the D/deaf clients.

The physical environment should be arranged so that the interpreter signs in front of a contrasting wall or backdrop. A blackboard or divider of appropriate color can make a good background, or one can hang fabric of contrasting color behind the area where the interpreter will be working. In hanging the fabric or backdrop, remember to have it wide enough to frame the interpreter from several angles. A common error is to place the backdrop directly behind the interpreter, without precautions being taken for D/deaf viewers not sitting directly in front of the interpreter.

REMOVABLE BACKGROUND FABRIC

CURTAIN

MOVABLE PARTITION

SOLID COLOR WALL

Lighting

Another factor to be considered in the positioning of the interpreter is lighting. It is essential that the interpreter be placed in a location which permits the best possible light on the face and hands. There should not be a bright light source behind or from below the interpreter, such as a window, open door or lamp, shadowing or distorting facial expression. This is also true in the case of the D/deaf people involved. It is difficult to interpret from sign to voice if the signer is in front of a light source or poorly lit.

Lights can be important in other ways, as for example, in movies when the lights are low or off. On these occasions it is helpful to have a pocket flashlight, which the D/deaf client holds on the interpreter as the film is being interpreted. Some rooms have dimmer switches or lights which can be set at a comfortably low level for viewing both the movie and the interpreter. If you're caught without a flashlight, or if the batteries are dead, there are some last-minute solutions as well, such as leaving the door slightly ajar to let in a bit of light, using a partially covered overhead projector, a tensor lamp, or an orchestra lamp. At a site which has interpretation regularly, a lighting solution should be implemented using an appropriate light source.

Appearance

There are many little details to be attended to for a truly professional appearance. Hair is off the face; beards and mustaches should be carefully (and honestly) assessed for their possible distraction level. Certainly, facial hair is always trimmed around the lips well enough for ease in speechreading. Makeup is moderate, although many people feel that lipstick is a must for speechreading from any distance, especially in platform situations. Nails are not too long, and neutral nail polish can be used, if any is used at all. Glasses should fit well enough so that they do not fly off the face or need constant attention and adjustment. No jewelry is worn that might be noisy or distracting. Gum is never chewed while on the job. Many people believe they can hide their gum. Gum hidden in the mouth can alter appearance, facial expression and facial grammar.

Clothing

Clothing should be appropriate for the occasion. If the interpreter is planning to interpret in court, it is helpful to know that some judges still require women to wear dresses. By contrast, wearing a dress may be inappropriate for a class-room situation where the interpreter must work around machines, such as a welding or printing class. For interpreting during a job interview the interpreter tries to be only an asset and not a liability to the clients involved. If the interpreter is not dressed appropriately this might lead the employer to believe that the prospective employee does not command respect, or vice versa. Simply stated, the interpreter should dress in a professional manner that suits the environment and which brings honor to the profession. People respond to the way we look and make decisions about competence, trustwor-thiness and status based on appearance. Interpreters might do well to consider this in their dress and appearance.

The interpreter dresses conservatively in order to be as respectful and unobtrusive as possible and to provide the best possible background for signing. Excessive makeup, noisy or distracting jewelry, and excessive detail in clothing can all be distracting. The basic criteria to use in assessing appearance is that the interpreter should be the least obtrusive person in the room and should provide a comfortable, readable background for signing.

Body Language, Facial Expression and Facial Nuance

Because they typically encounter people who do not use their language, D/deaf people often depend heavily on body language and facial expression to understand their surroundings. Perhaps this knowledge can help interpreters remember to consider these factors carefully in the interpreting process. Interpreters must be sure that they are communicating precisely what is intended through the facial and body modes. A sense of insecurity can turn a statement in the source text into a question in the interpretation, for example, if the interpreter has a questioning look when wondering if something is being signed correctly.

To carry the true intent and spirit of the source text, the interpreter must use nonverbal as well as verbal cues to produce that semantic intent in the target language text. Many of the subtleties of communication, such as sarcasm, jokes, and innuendo depend heavily on the nonverbal level. We must find effective ways to convey the same nuances through facial and body expression and from the visual form to a voiced form. Many of the techniques of pantomime can be useful in sending nonverbal information. As a general rule, however, we are not pantomiming when we interpret, and pantomime would surely not be subtle enough for a typical interpreting situation. It is a good idea to keep subtlety in mind for the purpose of maintaining a low profile as an interpreter, thus remaining unobtrusive. Often people compliment and therefore reinforce interpreters for extreme expressiveness; yet it might be a higher compliment if there were no comments. This might imply that the interpretation was so natural that the client felt the speaker was actually signing or speaking and there was no interpreter present.

There are two kinds of expression in interpreting: one is the emotional aspect of the speaker's tone, which is the one we most quickly and easily identify, and the other is the expression which is a requisite aspect of the grammar of ASL. This second kind of expression is a little more difficult to describe, but includes the expressions that show change of topic, characterization, emphasis of points, questions, statements, or adjectival aspects of nouns and adverbial aspects of verbs, showing degree or quantity, such as HARDWORK versus WORK or shades, values and hues of a color. These expressions are modified within the sign or within the utterance without necessarily having a separate vocabulary item to represent that aspect. This is a property of ASL but can and should apply to transliteration as well on many occasions.

Reading of body language is an important skill of the Sign Language interpreter. The interpreter must find ways to express vocally the visual expression of the D/deaf person. The same rules for transmitting the spirit of the speaker apply in sign-to-spoken interpreting as in spoken-to-sign interpreting. For example, if the signer were to sign GOOD with limp body and hands and a sour expression, the interpreter might vocalize "kind of good" with a negative inflection in the voice.

The interpreter further uses receptive body language skills, back channel communication, to determine to some extent the comprehension of the D/deaf consumer and whether they are comfortable with the interpretation. One example of a visual indication that the D/deaf consumer is not comfortable with the use of particular lexical items is the mimicking of "new" signs with a look of confusion or a questioning look. If the D/deaf client does this several times during the course of an interpretation, the interpreter might recognize this as a cue to use older or more traditional signs. If, on the other hand, the D/deaf client often suggests "new" signs for fingerspelled words, or asks for the English equivalent of signs, this could indicate that this D/deaf person is interested in transliteration with an emphasis on English vocabulary rather than ASL vocabulary.

Eye contact is another factor in body language that should concern the interpreter. We need to maintain eye contact with

D/deaf persons for several reasons. With eye contact, the interpreter can tune in to the understanding and preferences of the
D/deaf client. The interpreter's energy is most effective in my
experience with powerful eye contact. Somehow the energy the
interpreter puts out recycles into the interpreter's system when
there is a strong connection with the client(s). Another reason
is that the D/deaf client can then feel the communication link
that eye contact can provide. Notice, however, the interpreter
should not have a staring contest with the D/deaf person, for
that will cause discomfort, but should simply maintain general
eye contact.

Because Sign Language is visual, it is essential that we pay
attention to our facial and body expression even more than we
do in communicating with vocal languages. The D/deaf person
has, in general, highly experienced eyes and will probably
receive the signer's body language first and then the speaker's
words. We are always communicating visual information, and it
is the task of the interpreter to be aware of what is communicated and to try to convey as accurately as possible
paralinguistic information, as well as the verbal information
that is transmitted through the signs, words and phrases chosen.

For an exercise in nonverbal expression, try to sign the
same sentence with different emotions and try to speak the
same sentence with varied expressions to see how much a
change in expression affects the meaning of an utterance. It
may be useful to do this in a group and discuss emotions that
are difficult to portray. Our faces and our bodies are made up
of muscles which, when exercised, can be very well developed
and controlled. Once we are sensitive to exactly what they are
doing and the effect of their movement in expression, we can
control the information we transmit.

Thought Questions

1. Why are visual physical factors important for interpreting?
2. List five aspects of placement that can influence ease of watching for a D/deaf person.
3. List three reasons for concern about placement in reference to the interpreter's needs and comfort.
4. Explain the importance of lighting in interpreting.
5. List five aspects of appearance that relate to a professional job of interpreting.
6. Why is dress important for an interpreter? What are some concerns to keep in mind regarding dress in different situations?
7. How do some people use body language other than while signing?
8. What are some subtleties of language that are expressed non-verbally?
9. Why is subtlety important in the interpreter's function as it relates to body language and facial expression?
10. List five verbs and at least five ways they can be modified within the sign to indicate variations in meaning. How can nouns be modified to include extra information? Adjectives? Adverbs?
11. What are the two kinds of expression that an interpreter should be aware of in transmitting information?
12. Why are body language and facial expression important in reading signers?
13. How and why is eye contact important in an interpreting situation?
14. What is the time frame for optimal interpretation? How long should an interpreter work without a break? What are the implications of this for teaming and turn-taking?

 Chapter 4

Orientation to the Deaf Community

The Deaf Community is a basic part of the lives of many D/deaf people. Interpreters need to be familiar with its workings in order to be: 1) more culturally aware and comfortable, 2) more knowledgeable about references made to various aspects of the community, such as acronyms for organizations or name signs for people who are well known in that community, and 3) constantly in a position to upgrade their functional language skills and to add new signs and structures to their receptive and expressive repertoire. The Deaf Community is an identifiable force in the world of many D/deaf and hearing individuals who are involved in that community in any capacity.

As in most closely knit communities, there is a very effective communication system known as the "grapevine." Through this vehicle much information is passed, both rumor and fact. It was often stated, jokingly, that any difficulty in the use of the telephone was no handicap for D/deaf people because their communication grapevine was so effective.

The Deaf Community consists of social units at many levels, from the family to an international organization. There is, at the international level, an organization known as the World Federation of the Deaf (WFD), which has regular conferences, and has many goals, but perhaps its most significant objective is the improvement of the life of D/deaf people around the globe. At the national level there are both professional and nonprofessional organizations of and for D/deaf people. Because of my circumstances, most of my examples are from the USA, but that is not to imply that such organizations exist only in this country. The National Association of the Deaf (NAD), is an umbrella organization for many other organizations, and is a major voice of D/deaf people in the United States today. Within the structure of the NAD are state chapters such as the California Association of the Deaf (CAD), and local chapters such as the Metropolitan Washington Deaf Community Center (MWDCC) and the Colorado Springs Silent Club (CSSC). The Alexander Graham Bell Association (AGB), is an organization established for those individuals with a preference for the oral mode. Professional national organizations include the Association of Visual Language Interpreters of Canada (AVLIC) which has local chapters throughout Canada and the Registry of Interpreters for the Deaf (RID), and its local chapters such as Southern California Registry of Interpreters for the Deaf (SCRID), and the Texas Society of Interpreters for the Deaf (TSID). These interpreter organizations have many Deaf members as well as interpreter members and supporting and student members.

Publications in the field include *The Deaf American Monograph* and *The Broadcaster*, both publications of the NAD; the *American Annals of the Deaf*, the official organ of the Conference of Executives of American Schools for the Deaf (CEASD) and the Convention of American Instructors of the Deaf (CAID); the *Volta Review*, the publication of the A. G. Bell Association; the *Journal of Rehabilitation of the Deaf*, published by the American Deafness and Rehabilitation Association (ADARA), and the *Vocational Rehabilitation Journal*, a general periodical in the area of rehabilitation that includes some articles on D/deaf people. There are national deaf-related newspapers like *The Silent News* and *Newswaves*, in addition to numerous local publications, such as the newsletters of various religious groups that are organized especially for D/deaf individuals, or which sponsor programs for D/deaf people. Also, local organizations and educational programs which have D/deaf students publish information that can be invaluable for keeping up on the activities of the Deaf Community. Many publications are now on the Internet, such as *Deaf Digest* and many organizations have added bulletin board and news sites.

The U.S. Office of Special Education and Rehabilitative Services (OSERS), under The Department of Education contains a section known as the Rehabilitation Services Administration (RSA). Most of us have contact with this broad governmental agency at the local level through the workings of the division known as Vocational Rehabilitation (VR). Often there is a rehabilitation counselor for the D/deaf (RCD), who specializes in D/deaf people.

Listed above is a far from comprehensive list of organizations, publications and agencies. Interpreters usually find it advantageous to investigate the various organizations of the Deaf Community in which they live and to become actively involved, if possible. As is true of any user of any language, it is essential to be associated with the community that uses that language in order to keep current in usage and vocabulary, and to be fully conversant with the cultural aspects of that community.

Like all languages, ASL is alive and changing. This is evidenced by the addition of such vocabulary as SPACE SHUTTLE, or ROCKET, which was needed when the space program began, or STREAKING, when that was a fad in the early 1970s and the plethora of terms associated with the computer age. By simply being involved with the Deaf Community, we are better able to stay abreast of these and many additional changes. Most of us also need a certain amount of practice in the use of ASL, and there is no better way than to maintain contact with D/deaf people from many walks of life. Community involvement provides this contact.

The education of D/deaf children is important in understanding the Deaf Community. Typically the education of D/deaf people is different in many ways from that of their hearing peers because of their different needs. There are three general types of educational programs for D/deaf people in the U.S.A. The education of D/deaf children in residential schools differs most significantly from the general education of hearing children. These institutions are usually run by the states in which they are located. D/deaf students typically live in dormitories and go to school on the same campus, although there are more and more children attending residential schools, but living at home with their own families. Often dialectal signs in certain states seem to originate in the residential schools, since historically the majority of signing D/deaf adults went through residential programs as children. Woodward (1973), has pointed out that long term attendance at a residential school correlates with fluency in ASL. This fact may assist the interpreter in situation assessment (see Chapter 2.) If there is a residential school nearby, it would be helpful to visit the school.

Another type of school program is the day school, which serves D/deaf students who commute to school daily. As might be expected, these programs tend to exist in larger cities. Day schools vary as to approach; many use Total Communication, usually MCE, others are oral. There are also schools employing a Bi-lingual/Bi-cultural approach in which students are taught ASL as well as English and are taught about the history and culture of Deaf people as well as about traditional history and culture. A third kind of educational program exists for D/deaf students in an integrated setting, where both hearing and D/deaf students attend the same school, which may or may not have special classes for D/deaf students and possibly certain integrated classes, depending on the needs of the particular D/deaf student. Programs of this last type are referred to as "mainstream" programs. Students from such programs may be more accustomed to the use of interpreters and/or may rely on MCE, or the Oral Method. Often these students are served by itinerant teachers, on site interpreters and/or a specialist teacher on site.

Ideally an interpreter can interact with the Deaf Community in both a formal and an informal manner. An interpreter could become formally involved in governmental and other civic or educational organizations serving or benefiting D/deaf people. Informally, an interpreter might like to discover where some D/deaf persons tend to spend their free time, or become involved in a sports activity that has been organized by D/deaf people. A Deaf club in the area would be an interesting place to visit. Some areas have homes for D/deaf senior citizens, religious programs, and other programs or institutions at which the new person attempting to join the Deaf Community might be interested in offering service and friendship. Often an interpreter can get a little realistic experience by interpreting for D/deaf people in a group residence, such as a dormitory. Resources vary in every individual community. We must be sensitive to avoid being intrusive invaders into someone else's world. Never forget the fact that these contacts are actual people with their own agendas and priorities. They may offer a wonderful opportunity, but that is not usually their reason for being. The most important thing is to find a productive way to associate with that community, and from the initial contact further contacts will become more readily available.

Thought Questions

1. What are three reasons that it might be beneficial for an interpreter to be aware of the Deaf Community?

2. What is another term for informal communication among D/deaf people?

3. Name some of the organizations of D/deaf people at different levels, both informal and formal.

4. Name three kinds of educational systems for D/deaf children in the United States of America.

5. Describe events and ongoing institutions in your local area where D/deaf people gather. Which of these could you visit?

Chapter 5

The Ethics of Interpreting

Most professions operate under a set of guidelines or a code of ethics. The Ball State Teacher's College Conference in 1964 marks the inception of the Registry of Interpreters for the Deaf (RID). At that conference, the Interpreter's Code of Ethics was established. That this Code of Ethics has undergone significant revision is an indication that interpreting is a growing profession (See Appendix A for the complete text).

For many reasons, a code of ethics is important to the interpreting profession. First of all, interpreters are in a unique position because they control the flow of information. The interpreter is often the only hearing person in a room who is bimodal/bilingual; therefore, an unscrupulous interpreter could alter what is communicated, with the possibility of going undetected. Thankfully, most interpreters are not unscrupulous. There are also people who do not think of themselves as unscrupulous, but function in an unethical manner, perhaps due to a lack of awareness or training. We need a code of ethics to give these possibly well-meaning but unethical individuals a framework for appropriate behavior.

It is essential that interpreters recognize the responsibilities of our profession to adequately protect the rights of D/deaf and hearing clients, along with our own rights. A code of ethics protects the interpreter and lessens the arbitrariness of one's decisions by providing guidelines and standards to follow. Sometimes, for example, the D/deaf or hearing client may ask the interpreter to take on more responsibility than the transfer of information. If the interpreter tells the client that this doesn't seem to be the most effective use of one's time, or that one is not particularly interested in that level of involvement, these responses can cause unnecessary resentment or confusion. The interpreter can, rather, explain to the clients that it is impossible to comply with a request because it conflicts with the Code of Ethics of the interpreting profession. When an interpreter acts solely as an individual and must justify every decision on the basis of personal standards, it is easier to falter and end up in an uncomfortable position.

The Code of Ethics also offers some consistency within the interpreting profession. Through our adherence to the Code of Ethics, our clients, both hearing and D/deaf, will know what to expect of us and what not to expect when they call upon us to serve them. This is a critical point; each of us paves the way for the rest who follow. The first interpreter that a person deals with can profoundly affect that person's attitude toward the interpreting profession. If we do a good job of educating clients, the next interpreter's job is then much easier, as the client's expectations are more likely to be appropriate. Initial contact seems to be a very strong influence on future behavior, so we must always try to be professional and ethical in order to educate the public properly as to our function.

Interpreting ethics involve the equalization of the communication experience for all people involved in a situation. This means that we are aiming for a condition in which the quality of the communicative experience is the same whether a person is D/deaf or hearing.

There are four general principles upon which the Code of

Ethics rests: confidentiality, impartiality, discretion, and professional distance. These will be covered individually below.

Confidentiality

Confidentiality involves the maintenance of privacy of the parties involved in a situation. Breach of confidentiality is probably the most serious offense an interpreter can commit. Confidentiality is so essential and so basic that, without it, the entire interpreting task might as well not occur. Confidentiality involves trust, and if this trust is lost, many other things are lost as well. If an interpreter cannot be trusted to keep confidences, then that person should not be entrusted with the responsibility of interpreting.

The interpreter is a third party and, regardless of how helpful and necessary to the communication process, remains an extra person. The individuals involved would probably prefer to deal with one another directly, removing the third person. Unfortunately this is impossible unless they share a language. If we can imagine how we would feel if we had to speak of intimate matters in the presence of an outside person, we might be just that much more sensitive to our privileged position as interpreters.

The RID has a system for enforcement of the Code of Ethics, a grievance procedure. However, beyond this formal level, if an interpreter breaks confidence, it can easily spread along the "grapevine" and that interpreter's reputation may be ruined in certain circles. On the other hand, the highest form of retribution is the self-respect that is lost by breaking the code of ethics.

Impartiality

Impartiality is a significant aspect of the Code of Ethics. The interpreter must remain neutral and not show personal feelings while interpreting. Interpreters cannot allow themselves to show their reactions to situations or to the information they are transmitting. We need to develop a way that we can release our feelings without revealing confidential information and without affecting the situation at hand. Perhaps we can "talk" to a stuffed animal, chop wood, or beat on a pillow; some people talk things out alone in the isolation of their cars on the way home. The relationship between mentor and mentee allows for discussion of feelings and situations within the confidentiality of both parties as does that between therapist and client. Whatever the strategy for dealing with our feelings, it is essential that we do so. If we allow our reactions to affect our functioning, we could easily bias the outcome of the event. For example, by interpreting more dramatically for one party than the other in a divorce, we could make one party look better than the other. Without being sensitive to this pitfall, it is possible to do the damage without being fully aware of it.

Impartiality means treating all parties equally. For instance, we must be impartial in eye contact with all D/deaf clients in a setting. It is easy to maintain eye contact with a very attentive client, but it is rather hard sometimes to keep up eye contact with a client who tends to look around or who simply looks less interested.

Interpreters need to treat all clients equally in other aspects as well. It is essential that we avoid siding with or even appearing to side with one client. Sometimes interpreters are asked or are tempted to play the role of advocate for D/deaf people. As individuals this is fine, even commendable; as interpreters we must keep our role clear that on the job we transmit information between clients. Another pitfall is that sometimes interpreters appear to be siding with either the hearing or the D/deaf client, perhaps because people view other people who share characteristics as "sticking together," i.e., "they're both hearing" or "they both sign." Thus, we must be careful, both in our attitudes and in our behavior. Don't tell one client the other can't follow because the conversation is going too fast; don't talk without signing or sign without talking to either client. These are examples of behaviors that could be viewed as indicating prejudice on the part of the interpreter. Simply by being aware of such behaviors and their implications, we can avoid much difficulty.

Sometimes we fall prey to ego and, because we feel it is a reflection on ourselves or our interpreting, are reticent to interpret a "stupid question" and in very subtle (or not so subtle) ways repress the participation of a client who regularly tends to ask what we view as stupid questions. Another pitfall, in the area of sign-to-spoken interpreting, relates to the skill level of the interpreter. Sometimes, when faced with a client who is difficult for that interpreter to read, the interpreter may, in effect, repress that person's participation so as not to be placed in the embarrassing situation of haltingly interpreting the client. The interpreter must make the atmosphere as comfortable as possible so that everyone will feel free to communicate, to express themselves, or not to express themselves. The interpreter must not block communication in any way.

Discretion

Discretion, or the use of judgment, is essential in many aspects of the field of interpreting. Being fully aware of one's abilities will allow the interpreter to turn down an interpreting job when not feeling skilled enough to accept a specific assignment. In some situations, the interpreter may be too personally involved with the individuals in the particular setting. Awareness of one's limitations and the conviction to act upon that awareness is evidence of discretion.

It is often said that "some service is better than no service at all"; however, this can be fallacious in the case of interpreting, for it can be argued that service was rendered symbolically, but not practically. When an interpreter has attempted too difficult an assignment, no one can claim that there was "no service," but for all practical purposes there was no service for the good that service did the consumers relying on the interpretation. If the under-skilled interpreter passes on erroneous information, it is possible that no one would catch this error; the parties involved could remain ignorant of it, leaving the communication worse than poor, for now it is deceptive. Another reason that a poor interpreter may be worse than no interpreter is that the person who attempts to do the job may tarnish the reputation and trust that professional interpreters have worked so very hard to build. We are seen as a group, not only as individuals, and what each of us does influences the attitudes people have toward us as a whole.

If the interpreter has difficulty interpreting in certain situations, such as those involving a very different philosophical view, then it is probably best to avoid such situations. Even in an uncomfortable situation, the interpreter would still be expected to do a professional job of transmitting the information presented. There is no excuse for the breach of ethics that altering the interpretation would represent. It is only human to be uncomfortable with situations that are foreign or in disagreement with our own sense of right and wrong; but it is the right of the consumers to determine their own sense of right and wrong, and to be exposed to whatever they choose in the manner it is presented. If the interpreter can maintain an impartial attitude, assignments such as these can be accepted and possibly even enjoyed.

As a general rule, we have many associations with D/deaf people. Sometimes we are called upon to interpret in situations in which we are very familiar with some of the parties. If the interpreter is too close to the people involved, then it would be best to suggest that another interpreter serve. It is always nice to offer to help to find another interpreter and to explain the reason behind the refusal to interpret so as to maintain good relations. We may not do a thoroughly professional job interpreting for a parent, spouse, significant other, child, close friend, enemy or any other person who has too much of an impact on our lives, or when the situation is such that the outcome might affect the interpreter as well as affect the client. It is even difficult to do justice to the task when there are no personal repercussions, but one's feelings toward the individuals involved are strong.

If, for example, one were asked to interpret for one's parent's divorce or that of a close friend, it would be extremely difficult to maintain any form of impartiality. Once an interpreter was interpreting for her grandfather's funeral and spent the entire time wishing that she were not the "cause" of her father's tears. Funerals create enough emotional stress for the interpreter without the added complication of being related to the parties involved. Sometimes it is helpful simply to know you have the right to turn down an interpreting assignment.

There are several considerations in accepting volunteer status: could the interpreter be paid if someone would do some legwork and find a funding source; would taking this position on a volunteer basis set a bad precedent; does the interpreter wish to volunteer; and is the interpreter able to remain professional regardless of the volunteer status of the interpreting? Often people resent feeling beholden to anyone and might really prefer to pay for the services of an interpreter or have the interpreting paid for by some other means. Certainly there is a great need to educate the public as to our role and as to the rights of individuals to participate in their world with professional services to facilitate their participation. Volunteering is optional and should be handled as a choice rather than as an expected service. Interpreters should not allow themselves to feel pressured into interpreting when they may later resent it.

Professional Distance

Professional distance is the quality of caring about the clients one serves without allowing that to interfere with one's interpreting function, nor letting one's knowledge or information about clients affect one's outside life. We must be certain that the client who meets us at a social gathering does not spend the whole time wondering if we are acting differently because of our prior knowledge. Imagine the feelings of a D/deaf person at a Deaf club meeting, for example, who meets the interpreter who was serving that afternoon in court for a hearing at which he was accused of infidelity to his spouse. It would certainly be an uncomfortable feeling in the first place, but would be even worse if the interpreter talked about the afternoon's experience, winked or gave some other indication that the two of them shared a naughty secret.

Similarly, our reaction to students' grades or response to a presentation or behavior of a client could be extremely inhibiting. If a student received a failing grade and the interpreter saw the grade, that might be embarrassing enough, but if the interpreter commented on it, that would surely worsen the embarrassment. By blushing at a client's behavior, we color the situation.

Another example of why professional distance is important is in the mental health setting. For instance, while waiting with a client for an appointment with a therapist, it is tempting to converse about the upcoming event. If such conversation were to occur, it is very possible that, having unloaded feelings, the client might be less able or willing to do so again in the therapy situation. Some consumers, unsophisticated in the use of an interpreter, might be tempted to ask the interpreter to recap the conversation or to fill in gaps. Neither is tenable. Finally, this puts the interpreter in the difficult situation of holding information. It might be tempting to give advice, help or it simply might be difficult not to be able to react and interact within and after the counseling situation.

We are highly involved in any interpreting assignment. The important concept is to avoid allowing our involvement to become inappropriate.

Ethical Conduct

The first contact with consumers can set the stage for the entire interaction. Always be sure to introduce yourself to the parties involved when entering a new situation, so that every one knows who you are and why you are there. The introduction should be concise and clear, stating your name and, if needed, the function of an interpreter. It may also be wise to mention the referring party, if there is one.

The four areas discussed help us to have a good overall idea of the code of ethics. In order for the Code of Ethics to have meaning, interpreters must understand and be able to explain or even defend its principles. Professionals cannot blindly follow a set of rules.

In order to maintain both the Code of Ethics and our public relations role, we must exercise tact. Often, out of ignorance, an individual will ask the interpreter for confidential information or to step out of a professional role. Even if the action is deliberate, the interpreter is probably much better off handling the whole affair as if it were not premeditated. When asked to step out of our professional role, the temptation is often to bark at the offender or to act self-righteously. It is probably best to gently but firmly explain the reason for refusal to agree to the request. When in doubt, educate. Another solution, of course, is to quickly change the subject or in some other way divert attention from the uncomfortable topic.

Central to the principles of ethical behavior is the necessity for interpreting faithfully the thought, intent and spirit of the people involved. The interpreter cannot alter the information or style for entertainment purposes, to help someone out, or because of personal opinion. The essential goal in interpreting is to make the situation equal, that is, an equal communication experience for the hearing and D/deaf people involved. By interpreting everything that is said and signed, all participants have access to communication and are appropriately exposed to the interpreter's function.

It is possible that the people involved might expect the interpreter to allow side comments or other information to pass. It is important to make it clear that the interpreter interprets everything, so that people do not act under erroneous assumptions. The interpreter might need to advise all parties in advance that everything will be interpreted. This is especially true in situations involving consumers who are unsophisticated users of interpreting services. Perhaps an introductory remark would be in order. The interpreter might say "My name is Mary Smith. I will be interpreting today. I will sign everything that is spoken and vocalize everything that is signed."

The interpreter is further called upon to avoid reacting to the content or style of the speaker or signer, so that the people relying on the interpreter for the information can form their own opinions. Some people react negatively to certain styles of presentation or to particular personalities. This can also be true for the information presented. Perhaps the real solution to not appearing judgmental is to try not to be judgmental while interpreting. Sometimes the concentration required helps not to show reactions by being too busy interpreting. To some degree it is possible to train oneself not to react. This training is evident in certain cultures in which a person must suffer a trial by pain without showing any reaction. In our own culture, people who are trained to be experimental observers develop the ability not to react so as not to effect an experiment while noting behavior.

There are many aspects of adherence to the Code of Ethics. Some general pointers to keep in mind are listed below. In discussing any aspect of interpreting, the interpreter must be certain to avoid naming people involved, places, dates, situations in detail, or any other particulars. It is possible that what may seem a very limited amount of information could be enough, if combined with another person's limited knowledge, to break confidentiality. Therefore, we must be cautious about sharing even what may seem to be unimportant or unenlightening facts. For example, if an interpreter were to say "Last month I interpreted for a divorce case, and the husband had to take three days off work. That's hard when you are a part-time worker, since they deduct from your paycheck." The previous sentences may seem relatively harmless, but there is danger in almost every word. Specifying the time, "last month," may be just the clue that lets someone know who was involved, along with the information that it was a divorce case. The facts that the husband had to take three days off work, that he has a part-time job and that money was deducted from his paycheck might be the information that would clearly tell someone exactly who was involved. A further complication is that it may be that the people involved would not wish people to know some of the details specified, such as the fact that the husband had to take three days off work, or that his job was part-time, or that they were getting a divorce.

Interpreters need to support one another. So often, people who do not understand the role or function of an interpreter will complain or gossip about the inadequacy of one interpreter to another interpreter. Sometimes this can be flattering to the person confided in; however, it is still important to maintain our faith in our colleagues. Often a misunderstanding causes such complaints, and we might be able to resolve the misunderstanding by clarifying the interpreter's role or by referring the complainer back to the interpreter involved.

Along this same vein, interpreters should try to discourage consumers confiding in them. We should not be the holders but the transmitters of information. If a consumer, for example, were to confide in the interpreter before an interpreting situation, that consumer might be tempted to ask the interpreter to then repeat the information to the other person involved in the interpreting situation.

If asked about some aspect of D/deaf people, we should not think of ourselves as experts but rather refer the interested party to people who are experts. We are experts in communication and are able to answer many questions about communication and interpretation, but we should avoid acting as experts in areas such as psychology, law or education. Posing as experts also relates to giving advice. This can be dangerous. If we give advice, we might be given the responsibility for ensuring action, so it is probably best to try to give as little advice as possible. So often we are seen as a good source of information because we are involved in many different aspects of people's lives, including the interpretation of information from an expert, and may appear to know about the information being presented, since we function as the "hands" or "voice" of the expert. We share both parties' language and are usually therefore easier to talk to. This leads to temptation on the part of the client to turn to us for advice.

Thought Questions

1. Explain why the code of ethics is important to our profession.

2. The underlying philosophy of the code of ethics is equal communication access. Give some examples of how the code could help to ensure equality in communication for all persons involved.

3. What are the four major areas covered in the code of ethics?

4. Why are these four areas important to the rights of D/deaf people?

5. How does the Code of Ethics protect interpreters?

6. How would you handle a question from another interpreter about the outcome of a court case you had been interpreting? Why would you take the steps you outlined?

7. How would you handle a question from a friend who saw you at the courthouse about the outcome of a court case you had been interpreting? Why would you take the steps you outlined?

8. How might an interpreter avoid showing feelings of disapproval in an interpreting situation?

9. List some of the general points to keep in mind as an interpreter in thinking about the Code of Ethics.

10. How does the interpreter determine what information from a specific interpreting assignment can or cannot be shared?

11. What is an area in which an interpreter is expert?

12. List four considerations in accepting compensation or serving as a volunteer.

13. On what occasions might an interpreter refuse to work on a volunteer basis?

14. What would you do if you were interpreting for a group therapy session and its members asked you to participate?

15. How would you handle a lecturer who used foul language?
16. List some situations that might be complex or difficult to handle. Using these situations, role play possible solutions.

Chapter 6

Sign-to-Spoken Interpreting

There is limited justification for a separate chapter on sign-to-spoken interpreting. The function of interpretation itself does not alter from English or into English. Sign-to-spoken interpreting is no harder than spoken-to-sign interpreting, but hearing audiences, being generally less exposed to interpreters, rely differently on the interpreter than the average D/deaf audience. Because D/deaf clients are probably much more accustomed to receiving information through an interpreter, they are probably also able to watch interpreters with more ease and flexibility. Sign Language interpreters are expected to put what they see into appropriate and precise English. This is another reason that the interpreter's command of both languages is important. Development of ASL and English vocabularies and grammatical principles cannot be overemphasized.

Many interpreters feel that one of the ways they develop their sign-to-spoken skills is through frequent association with the Deaf Community because in this way they are exposed to natural language use and can practice the task of reading and understanding signs. Reading and actually transforming signed expressions into vocal expressions are, however, very different tasks. Receptive skill is essential to sign-to-spoken interpreting, but the actual task must be practiced to develop successful interpretation. Effective sign-to-spoken interpreting is essential for D/deaf people to actively participate, contribute and respond rather than being only passive participants. We must work to make their expression as eloquent, or ordinary, in the vocal medium as it is in the visual.

Sign-to-spoken interpreting is often conveyed simultaneously. First person is typically used, meaning that if the signer says "I want you to go over there," the interpreter will vocalize in the same person, "I want you to go over there." First person is typically used in consecutive interpretation, but occasionally third person is applied to the interpretation. The default has been first person. Third person is used when there is confusion as to who the source of information is or when circumstances suggest that as the more effective approach. With the same stimulus statement as above the interpretation would be, "He wants you to go over there" or "Tom wants you to go over there" or "Dr. Simms wants you to go over there" or "Mr. Simms wants you to go over there".

Visibility is always an essential factor in the planning of seating of the involved parties. The interpreter must be able to clearly see the signer and be seen by the people relying on the signed interpretation. When a signing speaker is on a stage or such, probably the best vantage point for the sign-to-spoken interpreter is in the audience in front of the signer, with a microphone if necessary. Just as the spoken-to-sign interpreter should not be placed in front of a light source, so should the interpreter make certain that the signer is not in front of a light source, that there is sufficient lighting, and that there are no distractions.

It is important to speak loudly enough to be heard clearly even when your back is to the audience, yet not too loud for comfort. Interpreters should be careful not to mumble; rather they should pronounce loudly, clearly and carefully, unless the signer visually mumbles or whispers. A microphone is more necessary for interpreters than speakers because the interpreter is generally facing the front rather than the audience.

The sign-to-spoken interpreter should remain as unobtrusive as possible. To some degree the interpreter is visually quiet, rather than contributing extraneous visual information. Care should be taken not to draw attention visually or vocally. Rather, the voice should be modulated to the comfort level of the listeners and to the spirit of the signer and the posture should be neutral and non-intrusive.

Sometimes interpreters copy signs of the signer while interpreting. This habit of mimicking can be very distracting. Within the signing population such behavior is often reserved for requests for repetition or clarification. For example, if the speaker signed "MY HOUSE THERE SMALL TOWN UPSHIRE," a reader could imitate the sign SMALL and the speaker might respond with "SMALL, 500 MAYBE 600 PEOPLE." If the reader imitated the sign TELEPATHY in an utterance like "MY FRIEND, ME TELEPATHY," the signer might spell MENTAL TELEPATHY, or explain its meaning. Interpreters can use this knowledge in order to request repetition of a particular sign and as a precaution against using this technique inappropriately.

Some speakers have prepared speeches. If this is the case, ask for a copy and study it ahead of time; then synchronize the voicing with the signing. The eyes of the interpreter must nonetheless be on the signer so that if the signer changes thoughts or interjects comments not on the paper, this can be interpreted. If no written paper is available prior to the presentation, perhaps the interpreter can obtain a copy of the presenter's notes, outline or the like. A list of terms to be used would be helpful in the absence of a more thorough preview. Some speakers might want or be willing to practice their speeches ahead of time and will allow the interpreter to practice with them. If there is the opportunity, it is wise to be as well prepared as possible; however, interpreting is a task of the moment and the interpreter must be prepared for any unplanned alterations in the presentation.

Choice of words and completeness are important skills for the sign-to-spoken interpreter. The interpreter should let the signer lead sufficiently to be able to make sense of what is signed and to give the appropriate vocal expression and rhythm. If the signer emphasizes one thought, the same emphasis should appear in the interpretation. The interpreter should strive to choose the most appropriate vocabulary for the meaning and tone presented.

There are many aids in the selection of appropriate English equivalents for signed concepts. In making style choices, we should consider the age, sex and social class of the signer, and the setting can be of some assistance. One might imagine a middle-aged woman saying "delightful," but not "Mamma mia!" and a little boy saying "gosh" or "gee" or "wow," rather than "Oh, my dear Lord!" Cultural and environmental clues can be very helpful, yet the interpreter must in the end rely on one's own sense of appropriateness in choice, because stereotypical responses only work in many, but not all, cases. There could be an occasional little old lady who might say "far out," or a bright child who could easily possess an erudite vocabulary beyond his or her years.

Lipreading is an essential skill for the sign-to-spoken interpreter. It can help to make a much more precise interpretation and can often help the interpreter out of difficult situations when an unfamiliar sign appears. It can also assist in the reading of fingerspelling. Allow the facial and throat movements of the signer to assist in your interpreting and learn to trust and use your lipreading skills. Naturally, this hint is only for augmentation of the linguistic comprehension. Many ASL signs and phrases have facial and lip markers that would not equate to an appropriate English translation of their meaning value.

Grammar is also important. The sign-to-spoken interpreter

should use appropriate grammatical structures when vocalizing. One challenging grammatical structure is tense. Because ASL and English have very different ways of handling tense, this frequently results in errors in sign-to-spoken interpreting. Maintain the appropriate tense throughout the utterance. For example, if the signer relates a childhood story and mentions wanting an ice cream cone, this should be spoken in the past tense, not "I want an ice cream cone." In ASL the past tense was established by the fact that the story is about the individual's childhood, i.e., "back when...." . Where structures are quite different between ASL and English, the challenge may be greater, especially in simultaneous interpretation. For example, rhetorical questions are much more prevalent in ASL than in English and passive voice is used in English regularly, while in ASL that semantic function is handled completely different. Clearly the interpreter must be sophisticated in the grammar of both English and ASL in order to do a smooth interpreting job.

Nonverbal Cues

The sign-to-spoken interpreter must be aware of the nonverbal elements of communication. Interpreters should be cautious not to show their own anxiety through body and facial expression. This is important for the client's confidence in the interpreter. Facial and body expressions associated with discomfort can sometimes be misinterpreted as disapproval or anger. It is important so that the interpreter is not misread as disapproving of the signer's utterances. This could seriously affect the signer's comfort. In a similar manner, the facial expression that accompanies concentration, can be interpreted by the viewer as negative. For the sake of a comfortable atmosphere, we must be acutely aware of the nonverbal messages we send, even when sign-to-spoken interpreting.

Vocal inflection and expression are also important in

sign-to-spoken interpreting. Interpreters should match the tone of the source text. Here again a high level of fluency in English and ASL is essential, so that the sign-to-spoken interpreter selects the appropriate English equivalent for a sign. As mentioned earlier, vocalization should fit the signer's age, sex, social class, style, appearance, personality, and so forth. Beyond selection of vocabulary, slang usage and colloquial expressions, the interpreter will make nonverbal vocalizations based on information regarding the signer. Sometimes a giggle will be a less appropriate vocalization than a guffaw or a chuckle. Certain expressions may call for a vocal "huh?" or "let me see," or a laugh or a gasp, for example. These would be chosen to match the individual producing the source text.

Ethical Considerations

The ethics of sign-to-spoken interpreting are the same as for the overall ethics of the field; however, some points should be emphasized here. We must remember not to react either to the user's information or to ourselves, such as when we make an error. If an error is made, it is probably best to correct it as quickly as possible and leave it at that. Too much apology can be intrusive and destroy the point of the speaker as well.

When the signer tells a joke, it may be appropriate for the interpreter to laugh, or giggle, but that laugh should be held until the end of the utterance, so that all the hearing participants will understand the joke before they hear any laughter.

Neither correct the signer nor add information to the spoken portion that is not expressed in the signed portion. We must transmit the words and spirit of the source text, which means being aware of vocal inflection and the body language and facial expression of the signer. In every interpreting situation we must transmit everything, even ideas, words and emotions which are not comfortable for us, such as swear words and anger, and topics that we sometimes feel strongly about.

Because the experiences of members of the Deaf Community and those of members of mainstream hearing society differ, cultural mediation is an essential part of the task of interpreting between individuals of different cultures. What this means is that information may not all appear on the surface of any particular utterance. Much information is assumed or even unconsciously held. Therefore, for true communication to take place, the interpreter must make that underlying information known in a form understood by the receiving party.

Never criticize the signer as an excuse for a poorly executed interpreting job. This is sometimes tempting, but merely seems like "sour grapes" and puts the D/deaf person in a poor light. If the interpreting job was difficult, regard it as a challenge and maintain a professional exterior.

Sign-to-spoken interpreting allows D/deaf people and hearing people the opportunity to interact more fully. We must develop skills and confidence, as well as comfort, in order to fill the need. As our skills grow, so will the quality of interchange and the comfort of those we serve.

Thought Questions

1. How can a sign-to-spoken interpreter remain unobtrusive? List four ways.
2. What are four influences in determining the English word or phrase that should be chosen for the interpretation?
3. What is the benefit of allowing the signer some lead time in sign-to-spoken interpreting?
4. List five physical considerations in sign-to-spoken interpreting.
5. List and discuss six ethical considerations of sign-to-spoken interpreting.

6. How can the sign-to-spoken interpreter best transmit the facial expression, body language and other nonverbal aspects of the signing in the vocalization of the signer?

Chapter 7

Interpreting in Various Settings

All interpreting situations involve the code of ethics and the basic principles of the field. In this chapter we will look at some of the special considerations of common situations in which interpreters find themselves. These settings are as varied as the people we serve; yet we will try to discuss some of the more general points, keeping in mind that they may vary with each client.

Religious Settings

Interpreting in the religious setting may include any number of experiences, from a simple religious service to a baptism, counseling session, wedding, funeral, bar mitzvah, or any number of other events. Often, interpreting in the religious setting involves an audience rather than one-to-one interpreting. It is important to assess the audience for sign system preference. One likely choice might be ASL, since one cannot predict the makeup of a congregation or because the people might represent a mixture of systems. Be sure to check for signs used in the particular setting, as certain signs vary according to their semantic value as used in different sects or religions. For example, "baptize" is signed differently by Catholics and Baptists, and Jews have a different sign for "Bible" than Christians. If you check ahead, you can save yourself confusion or embarrassment. Good resources would be an experienced interpreter, literature regarding signs for that particular church, or a D/deaf member of that faith.

One commonly finds music in the religious setting. Interpreters must be prepared to interpret hymns and the like. If possible read the appropriate section from a hymnal or songbook ahead of time and/or practice with the singer or choir, whether the program is live or taped. Work to express meaning and rhythm. Some interpreters leave the hymnal or music open in front of them in case they need to refer to it for words that are difficult to hear and to be ready for upcoming lines. When using such aids, try to continue giving the audience some eye contact.

RELIGIOUS INTERPRETING: TWO DIFFERENT POSITIONS

If a second language such as Hebrew, Arabic, or Latin is used, the interpreter is not generally expected to translate. Typically the interpreter signs "Hebrew word (or language)" or "Latin word.... " If someone knowledgeable has prepared an English translation for the interpreter, or if a translation is available in the prayer book or other literature, then the interpreter can follow the translation to sign to the audience while the other language is being spoken. Again, try to maintain some level of eye contact with the audience while reading. The interpreter may prepare translations of the work if familiar with the language involved or work from simultaneous text.

Some or all of the sermon or service might be prepared ahead of time, in which case an interpreter may have the luxury of looking over those portions before the event. This can be especially helpful for reading through any passages to be used from the Bible, Torah, Koran, or the like. Such passages may involve complex or poetic language, and preparation can assist in clearer interpreting.

The religious setting can be a forum for many strong feelings. Since interpreters must always be true to the spirit of the speaker, it is for emphasis that we mention the following again. It is essential for the interpreter to transmit feelings accurately in the interpretation. It might be wise to avoid interpreting in a situation where the emotions of the interpreter might be too strong to allow the spirit of the speaker to flow through the interpreter.

Television and Artistic Performances

More and more segments of life are becoming accessible to D/deaf audiences, including such things as television and theatrical events. Songs and plays are performed in Sign Language, plays and concerts are interpreted. Even television news, interviews, and other programs sometimes include an interpreter.

Live artistic interpreting requires generally larger signs for visibility, and often signs are chosen for their aesthetic value, as well as for their meaning. Often interpreters in artistic settings need to practice ahead of time and interpret simultaneously with the spoken or sung text.

A greater amount of latitude is given an artistic interpreter to provide opportunities for creativity. The interpreter first decides upon an interpretation of the meaning of the piece and then upon how to sign that meaning. Individual situations will dictate how much or little freedom the interpreter has in determining the interpretation. Deaf interpreters are actively working in this setting as well as Deaf consultants who assist in the translation and who help interpreters study the effect of their translation choices.

INTERPRETING FOR LIVE PERFORMANCE

In certain art forms, such as poetry and music, rhythm will also play an important role. Interpreters may alter their interpretation slightly to accommodate the rhythm. Meaning is still most important and accommodations for rhythm, beauty, or impact should not alter or obliterate the meaning.

Television interpreting is a particularly challenging form. Timing is stringent. When the camera cuts to commercial, the interpretation must be finished or it will be cut regardless. Therefore strategies for processing and lag time are unique in this setting. Often the material is prepared and rehearsed so that ending can be simultaneous. When that is not possible, the interpreter makes decisions based on audience comprehension and a sense of completion in order to effect a close at the same time as the televised text. Unless people are watching a huge television, the interpreter can be a very small image on the screen; therefore visibility can be difficult. If the interpreter is in an insert, one important precaution is keeping the interpreter's hands within the insert. Camera technicians are not always aware of the significance of an interpreter's hands and may cut out an important aspect of a sign. It might be wise to have a signer-adviser to watch and be sure the technicians don't cut out anything significant.

TELEVISION INTERPRETING: THREE APPROACHES

Since we never seem terribly large on television, it is important to sign and fingerspell clearly and as largely as is possible for the space at hand. It is sometimes suggested that one "cramp" one's signs in order to allow the camera to move in closer. In this way the interpreter will appear larger. It is helpful to work with the camera crew. Interpreters need to learn about camera work, and camera operators need to learn about the work of the interpreter in order for both to be more effective.

Medical and Mental Health Settings

Medical and mental health interpreting are very sensitive areas. Confidentiality, as always, is important, but may take on even further significance due to the personal nature of medical and mental health care.

Sometimes the sex of the interpreter may be an important factor, as the client may feel more comfortable with an interpreter of the same gender. Caution and tact are imperative: interpreters must never react to the client or situation. Occasionally the medical or mental health problem may be shocking, unattractive, or embarrassing. Although internally one might react, it is essential not to stare (i.e., at the anatomical area being examined) or react visibly. If swearing or shocking language or content occurs, the interpreter must be prepared to transmit without reacting.

Pantomime or graphic gesturing may be useful techniques, but here again interpreters must exercise caution. Pointing at parts of the client's body should be avoided. It may be better to rely on pictures, picture books or three-dimensional models so as not to embarrass or degrade the client. Another strategy is to create the section of the body being discussed on the hand or in space and refer to that constant as a pro-form. Generally, interpreters should avoid touching clients while interpreting.

Because information can be technical, unless the interpreter is trained in medical terminology, vocabulary should be handled cautiously. First, the interpreter should listen carefully, and any technical or unfamiliar words should be fingerspelled. The interpreter must not guess at meanings or even how to spell a word. It may be necessary to ask for repetition and/or for the spelling. Interpretation should avoid generalization. For example, "you have the flu" should not be signed "YOU SICK" but rather "YOU HAVE FLU." In the case where the client does not understand, the medical practitioner has the responsibility of explaining the condition. Preparation in specific medical terminology and practices can greatly improve interpreted outcomes.

Hearing patients do not always ask questions directly, sometimes they look confused or sound confused. Interpreters can simulate this natural interchange by transmitting confused facial expressions and half-copied words or signs into the vocal mode by saying "Huh?" or "flu?" without the consumer directly asking a question. It is not necessary to stop everything to formally ask a question. We often send messages through nods and questioning looks or remarks. It is important that the medical professional—not the interpreter—explain and answer any questions.

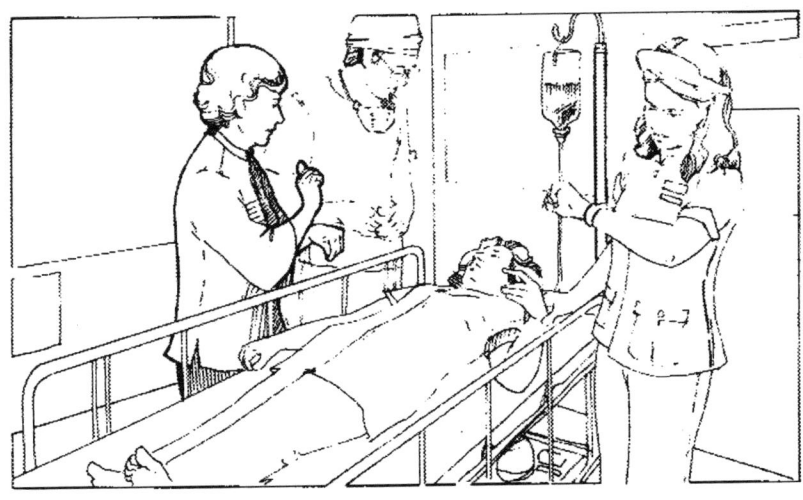

INTERPRETING IN THE MEDICAL SETTING

Several resources have listings of signs for medical situations. Woodward's <u>Signs of Sexual Behavior</u> and <u>Signs of Drug Use,</u> Fant's <u>American Sign Language Phrase Book</u>, Madsen's <u>Conversational Sign Language II</u>, Garcia's <u>Medical Interpreting,</u> and Costello's <u>Random House Webster's American Sign Language Medical Dictionary</u> are sources containing sections that pertain to terms that may come up in medical/mental health interpreting.

Mental health interpreting requires particular sensitivity to the fact that the interpreter may be an unwanted but necessary participant. Thus, using caution and tact is again essential. Interpreters must be careful not to appear to side with either therapist or client, and must also be cautious not to appear to assume the therapist's role. It might be necessary, and it's certainly helpful to explain the interpreter's role before beginning. At this time the client and therapist can be assured that the interpreter will transmit everything they say and that the interpreter will maintain confidentiality.

Sometimes consumers may use confusing language which may indicate their mental state. In these cases an interpreter needs to explain this to the therapist and interpret as accurately as possible without altering the client's language. It is essential here that the interpreter know the difference between ASL or some form of regular, common signing and poor or confused signing.

Sign-to-spoken skill is a necessary component so that communication is not stifled. If conversation prior to a situation is needed to orient the interpreter and consumer to one another's signing, it is important to avoid discussing mutual friends or acquaintances. Although it is natural to discuss the upcoming event, avoid such discussion as well. However, if the client is persistent, explain why you can't talk about the case.

Trust is a very delicate quality, and is easily broken. It is very important that no one view the interpreter as taking sides or becoming involved in any way; therefore the interpreter

INTERPRETING FOR A DOCTOR-PATIENT CONFERENCE
(MEDICAL OR MENTAL HEALTH SETTING)

must use caution in any conversations that take place in the view of the consumers. If the non-deaf person sees the interpreter chatting in a very friendly way with the D/deaf person, it may appear that the interpreter is biased toward the D/deaf person. The same can be said of the situation where the D/deaf person observes intimate-looking conversation between the non-deaf person and the interpreter.

In medical or mental health situations, it is possible that the interpreter might be tempted or even asked to handle questions related to D/deaf people; however, this can lead to confusion of roles and can be dangerous. The interpreter can try to have a list of resources handy so that clients can contact appropriate experts.

Platform Interpreting

Interpreters often serve at large meetings, lectures, banquets and other events where a speaker and audience are involved. Generally, the phrase "platform interpreting" is applied to any situation where the speaker stands in front of an audience in a relatively formal manner. If the speaker is communicating vocally, the interpreter generally stands nearby. On rare occasions the interpreter may sit in the audience facing the D/deaf portion of the audience. In these situations the interpreter should be seen without effort. If the presenter is signing, the interpreter is positioned in front and facing the signer, with a microphone if possible.

PLATFORM INTERPRETING

Usually the audience is farther away from the interpreter than usual, so physical factors are important. Signs are produced larger and fingerspelling is kept to a minimum. If a word must be fingerspelled, it should be done slowly and clearly. Hands must be kept slightly lower than usual if the interpreter is higher than the audience on a platform. This will allow facial information to be seen.

Background and lighting is also important. Interpreters should stand in the best light possible and in front of a solid, contrasting background. If there is any choice, of course, stand in a well-lit spot. It is helpful to have the light shining on the interpreter from several angles rather than full on the face only, shining into one's eyes. Also avoid lighting upward or downward over the face. Experiment with lights if this is unfamiliar to you. Posture can help visibility. Again, because the audience is lower, the interpreter's chin should not be set too high. Good posture can provide a better background for signs and a better basis to help one sign larger. Eye contact, as always, is important for maintaining rapport with the consumers and is helpful for assessing one's effectiveness. If the interpreter notices discomfort or confused looks, an adjustment in choice of style and/or signs may be necessary.

Larger signing and standing on one's feet can be fatiguing and, therefore, it is essential that platform interpreters only work for periods ranging from 15 to 30 minutes at a stretch, trading with other interpreters. If possible, trading should be done when speakers change, for this is far less distracting. When interpreters are working together taking turns, the one who is resting, along with backing up the primary interpreter, should watch for signs of fatigue and spell the fatigued interpreter when necessary.

If it is necessary to trade interpreters while a speaker is talking, the fresh interpreter moves behind the working interpreter, tapping the primary interpreter lightly to indicate readiness to take over. Then the fresh interpreter watches the working interpreter and listens to the speaker. When ready, usually at a discourse break, the working interpreter will move out of the way and the new interpreter will pick up where the first interpreter left off. This routine should be practiced until it is smooth, before it is done in front of an audience.

It is helpful to be familiar with the format of a program so that interpreting can be planned efficiently. If there are many speakers, it is helpful to know how many and approximately how long each will speak. In some cases an interpreter can stay on the platform through several speakers, knowing the speeches will be short. It is embarrassing to see a D/deaf speaker stand in front of an audience with no voice interpretation because no one can find the microphone. These factors should be attended to before the actual event.

Interpreters can prepare for platform interpreting by checking to see if speakers will use written speeches or outlines. If so, the interpreters can get a copy (or read over the speaker's copy if necessary) and study it ahead of time. It is sometimes useful to follow a signer's speech while sign-to-spoken interpreting. In that case, the interpreter should read over the speech ahead of time and then follow it with an eye constantly on the signer to permit the transmission of facial expression, side comments, digressions, and other details not in the written speech. The interpreter should watch the signer also to be sure the voiced and signed speeches are relatively simultaneous.

Platform interpreting requires more preparation and effort for visibility. Larger signing, solid backgrounds (as always), and good lighting can all contribute to more effective service.

Educational Settings

The legal and political climate in this country has led to more and more educational experiences being integrated. Residential schools for the D/deaf have vastly reduced populations. D/deaf and hearing students are taking classes from hearing and D/deaf teachers. This has caused an explosive need for educational interpreters. Because of this need, many interpreters have full-time interpreting jobs. Interpreters are present in many educational settings: elementary and high schools, junior colleges, adult education programs, four-year colleges and universities, masters and doctoral programs, vocational and technical programs, and less formal educational programs.

Generally, the interpreter sits facing the D/deaf student at the front, to the side and slightly in front of the teacher. If possible, the D/deaf student should be able to look past the interpreter to see the teacher without straining. This also applies to the use of visual aids. The interpreter should be positioned so as not to block visibility of visual aids and so that students can see both easily; sometimes this necessitates standing and moving around.

Since movement is so dominant in signing, interpreters should work to use space and directionality clearly and consistently. Whenever possible, preview any visual aids and determine the range and orientation. Range indicates such things as size of objects, amount of detail and focus of the material. Orientation refers to how the visual aid is orientated on the compass, what is to the right or left, and how things are situated on the up-and-down axis and so forth. If the visual aid is a movie or slides, low light should be allowed to shine on the interpreter. If no light has been arranged, a small flashlight can be held by the D/deaf student and used to light the interpreter's hands and face. Interpreters should carry such a flashlight with them.

EDUCATIONAL INTERPRETING: SECONDARY OT POST-SECONDARY

EDUCATIONAL INTERPRETING: ELEMENTARY OR PRESCHOOL

Typically, the educational interpreter specifically uses what-ever system is required by the educators in that setting. There may be a policy that requires use of one of the SEE systems in one school and ASL in another, or several systems, depending on the students or classroom. Since educators have additional responsibility regarding language development, they also tend to determine which system or systems are used. The interpreter will use whatever is required in a school. In colleges, universi-ties, junior colleges, and technical vocational programs, interpreters generally use the students' preferred language or system of communication. Again the institution's policy might dictate which way the interpreters lean. Often technical termi-nology comes into play and for this reason technical signs are used. Sometimes there is no known technical sign. In these cases the clients and interpreter may agree upon an invented sign to use for that term or may fingerspell it. Interpreters must remember that these may well be temporary signs, not useful or understandable with another client unless negotiated.

Sign Language interpreters are essential to access public education and are a vehicle for hearing and D/deaf individuals to interact.

Vocational Settings

Vocational interpreting may be defined as any interpreting in an occupational setting. An interpreter may be used when a D/deaf person is being hired or is hiring someone for a job, or when job preparation or on-the-job training is taking place. When the Department of Vocational Rehabilitation is involved with clients getting jobs, interpreters often serve that department in job counseling, testing or training situations.

Dress can be important in vocational interpreting. Scarves or loose skirts can be dangerous around certain machinery and clothes could get dirty in some cases. In an office setting, the jeans that were perfect around machinery may be quite inappropriate. Some people assume that the interpreter is a representative of D/deaf people, and they are certainly representatives of their colleagues, other interpreters. Ill-attired interpreters can harm such a person's attitude toward D/deaf people and/or use of interpreters in the future.

Technical terms may crop up that are familiar to people in a particular field but are new to the interpreter. Sometimes the interpreter can prepare by looking over books on a particular occupation. The signer may have a technical sign vocabulary that is greater than the interpreter, so the interpreter can pick up vocabulary from the client. While things are being demonstrated, it is a good idea to try to facilitate visibility by being as close as possible to the demonstration.

INTERPRETING FOR JOB INTERVIEW

INTERPRETING FOR VOCATIONAL TRAINING

Interpreting in vocational settings permits easy and comfortable communication between workers and management and among workers or among management, again allowing greater possibilities for inclusion. Some companies hire interpreters to work in their facilities full-time because they have so many D/deaf people in the firm.

Legal Settings

Any time the law is a factor, a situation could be called legal interpreting. This means interpreting where police are involved, in a courtroom, for attorney-client interviews, in jail or prison, with a probation or parole officer and so forth. Interpreters serve in both civil and criminal affairs. The National Registry of Interpreters for the Deaf has certification for legal interpreting, the Specialist Certification Legal (SC:L) (see Chapter 9, "Certification"). Legal interpreting requires knowledge of various legal settings, processes and terms, as well as skills in transmission of information.

Legal interpreters are sometimes called upon to explain their role for the court. If this is the case, be brief and respectful. Any time anyone is addressed in court, they must respond. This may merely mean stating that the interpreter is unable to answer a question.

Being audible takes on new meaning in court. One must be audible enough for the court reporter to hear and take down the words. The interpreter should consider this in positioning. If the interpreter's back is to the recorder, it is possible the voice will be muffled and difficult to hear.

Orientation to the signer's system of communication is essential, as always. Conversation with the client will allow the interpreter to become familiar with the client's signing and the client to become comfortable with the interpreter's signing.

COURTROOM INTERPRETING

INTERPRETING BETWEEN LAWYER AND CLIENT

It is still essential to avoid discussion of anything related to the case at hand, for confidentiality only applies when we are interpreting. If no third person is present, the interpreter can be asked to give evidence on information obtained during such a conversation. Tremendous caution is recommended in any case where the interpreter is alone with a client. Both to avoid conversation and simply for a rest, the interpreter may find it easiest to isolate oneself during breaks; however, be certain to stay close by in case you are needed.

Sign Language is highly visible. The interpreter can position oneself in such a way that signs are not visible to people other than the clients. Often lawyers and clients have quiet conversations in the hall outside the courtroom. It would be unfair if the interpreter signed so visibly that other signers could "eavesdrop" on the private conversation. In these cases the interpreter must exercise caution, signing in a whisper just as the lawyer speaks in low tones.

Terminology is an important factor in the legal setting. It is the lawyer's job to explain terms and legal consequences, but the interpreter must be prepared to clearly sign such explanations; therefore, familiarity with the terms and with the law is essential and will be of tremendous benefit to the interpreter. Likewise, the vocalization of information must be carefully handled. The interpreter works extra hard at accuracy and never assumes anything. It may be that responses are not necessarily coded in "signs" but may, in fact, be facial or gestural. If the D/deaf person nods, that is not vocalized as a "yes." The signer must use a sign that means YES. If a person gestures or points, the court interprets that vocally. For example, the judge may say, "the defendant is pointing to his right shoulder." The area of legal interpreting is complex and important. Interpreters would be well served by taking advantage of intensive legal training opportunities before working in this setting. Interpreters should be well prepared, competent and certified before accepting assignments in a legal setting.

Thought Questions

1. Which settings might generally require larger signing and minimal fingerspelling?

2. Which settings are generally one-to-one?

3. How can an interpreter prepare ahead of time for each of the settings described in this chapter?

4. How can interpreters handle music if it occurs in a religious or artistic setting?

5. How should an interpreter determine which language or sign system to use in each of the settings outlined in this chapter?

Chapter 8

Situations Calling For Special Skills

The stereotyped mental image of interpreting is an interpreter near a hearing speaker, facing one or more D/deaf persons. Other details may vary, but this is the general format. This chapter will deal with situations that don't quite fit this picture. We will be looking at telephone interpreting and interpreting where Deaf-Blind consumers, oral consumers or consumers with minimal language competence are involved. All of these cases require modifications of the ordinary interpreting format.

Telephone Interpreting

Since telephone interpreting is generally done on a one-to-one basis, the first thing to keep in mind is that the D/deaf client controls half of the event. The interpreter can ask the D/deaf consumer how to handle the situation. The D/deaf person placing the call can put the coin in the telephone or punch in a credit card number, dial the number, and, in effect, do everything necessary other than hearing on the telephone. Perhaps the D/deaf person also prefers to introduce the interpreter.

The interpreter should get in the habit of signing everything, as a telephone conversation provides no visual information for the D/deaf individual. Interpreters transmit the fact that the telephone is ringing, each time it rings, a busy signal, laughter, pauses, etc. In the same sense, the interpreter is responsible for conveying all the visual information, such as smiles, reactions, or other nonverbal visual information received from the D/deaf client.

Many D/deaf persons are quite sophisticated in the use of a telephone and a telephone interpreter. Some, however, are not fully aware of how to use an interpreter on the telephone; therefore, it might be helpful to clarify the options available. Some D/deaf clients use their own voices and may use the interpreter only as their ears while they speak for themselves. In such cases a speaker phone, earphones, a nearby telephone extension, or special equipment may be used. Other times the interpreter interprets in the more classic style between the two parties, typically using first person so that the two clients have a sense of talking to one another directly.

TELEPHONE INTERPRETING: DEAF PERSON NOT USING OWN VOICE

At the close of a telephone conversation, the interpreter should not hang up without being directed to do so by the D/deaf party, allowing time for the hearing and D/deaf clients to make any last remarks. Ideally the D/deaf person should tell the interpreter when to hang up, but if there is no direction, the interpreter should ask if both parties are finished before hanging up.

As technology moves ahead there will always be changes which allow D/deaf people to use the telephone or other devices more easily. Naturally, relay services allow D/deaf people greater flexibility in communicating with people who do not own telecommunication devices for the D/deaf. For those D/deaf people who prefer to read ASL rather than typed English, interpreters are employed in order to offer video relay services. Video telephones or other video reception equipment is required for such services. The interpreter then can work out of an office or even home (if they have the right equipment). Application of this type of service can be broader than telephone usage only.

TELEPHONE INTERPRETING: DEAF PERSON USING OWN VOICE

Oral Transmission

Although oral transmission is not Sign Language interpreting, it may be helpful to add a note about this sort of task, as it may be requested and because it may play a part in Sign Language interpreting. The oral task is the transmission of auditory input into the visual mode of lipreading accompanied by facial expression and body language. For optimum visibility, the face and neck should be clear of distractions, the hands should not cover any part of the face or neck, and the interpreter should be sure not to lean on the hands. In addition, the lighting should be good, especially on the face and neck. Scarves, lacy necklines, beards and mustaches can seriously reduce the visibility of the throat, lips and face for the lipreader. Another thing to be sensitive to is the color of the lips: they should be dark but not too bright.

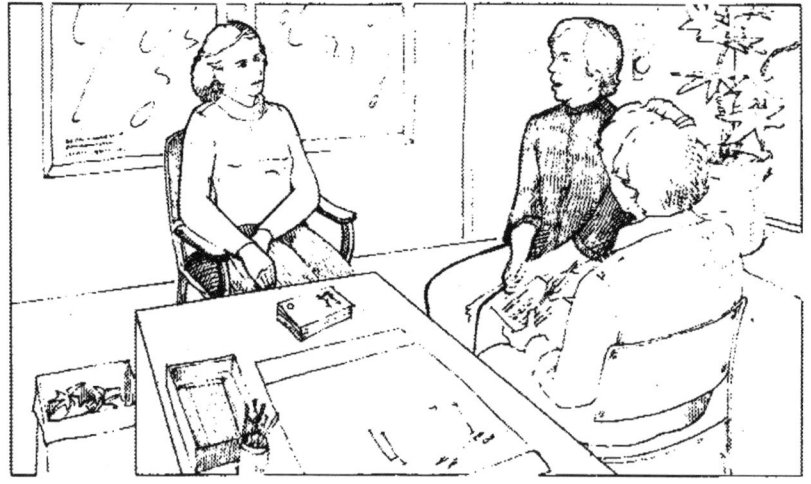

ORAL TRANSMISSION

Oral transmission requires close proximity for clear visibility. Typically the oral facilitator sits in front of the D/deaf consumers to be served and silently transmits, on the lips, what is spoken. Among the reasons oral transmitters are employed is because the speakers are often too far away for the oral deaf audience to lipread clearly. Another problem crops up when speakers move around, turn around and in other ways their faces become masked from the lipreader. There are further skills an oral transmitter develops for specialization in this area, such as synonym usage for words that are easier to lipread.[1]

Tactile Interpreting[2]

Many methods are used to communicate with Deaf-Blind and Blind-Deaf individuals. Depending on the initial state, that term is used first, so a person who is D/deaf and later loses vision is considered Deaf-Blind while a person who is blind and later loses hearing is considered Blind-Deaf. Communication will be influenced by the initial hearing status of the individual. A person who grew up hearing will have different needs and approaches than a person who grew up D/deaf and later became blind.

Tadoma is the technique of oral communication with a Deaf-Blind person through the use of the thumb on the lips for tactile lipreading and a finger on the throat to feel the vibrations of the vocal cords. Palm writing is a method in which one person draws out capital letters on the palm of the Deaf-Blind person to make words. A third method employs a special glove that has the letters of the alphabet in specific places on the palm. One person taps out words by pointing to the location of each letter on the glove. Some Deaf-Blind persons communicate by fingerspelling in one another's palms, while others sign and fingerspell in each other's palms. One other technique is to tap out the Morse code into the palm of a Deaf-Blind person, and another is to type to one another on a Braille typewriter that has six balls which raise and lower to create Braille that can be read at the moment it is being typed.

Some D/deaf people who are losing their vision or whose vision is not entirely impaired will grasp the other signer's wrists to follow the signing for assistance in focusing. With some forms of limited vision, the client can follow an interpreter carefully placed in their limited line of sight.

When using interpreters, Deaf-Blind individuals generally rely on tactile fingerspelling, tactile fingerspelling and signing, tactile typing, or the tracking described above, and sometimes prefer a combination of these techniques to avoid fatigue.

Tactile interpreting is necessarily almost always done on a one-to-one basis, and the interpreter must transmit not only what is audible but what is visible as well. This presents a great challenge and requires a good deal of judgment, as well as skill, sensitivity and awareness.

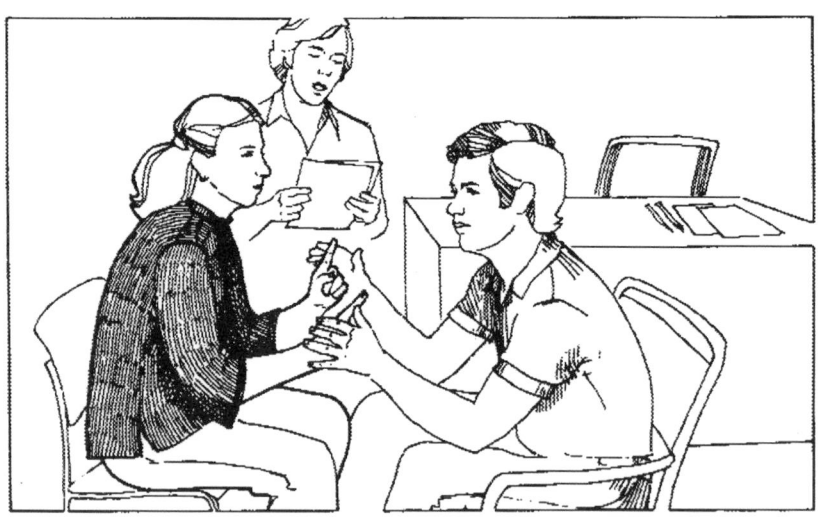

TACTILE INTERPRETING

Interpreting in a situation involving Deaf-Blind individuals can be challenging, both mentally and physically. There is an added weight on the hands of the interpreter, and the position of the signer may not be able to change as often or as easily as in other interpreting situations. The interpreter must be ingenious in finding ways to transmit visual and auditory input so that it is clearly readable and understandable. The interpreter must imagine how things will feel in the palm of the Deaf-Blind person and how to express things from one mode, the visual or auditory, into another, the tactile mode.

In interpreting situations involving D/deaf persons, an interpreter can usually adjust information, technique and style as a response to the visual input from the D/deaf consumers in the audience, however there is often little or no feedback from a Deaf-Blind consumer. Some Deaf-Blind individuals are not aware of the visual effect they have on others and do not emit ordinary visual signals; therefore, the interpreter must be prepared to determine the style, technique, and general approach based on other criteria, such as knowledge of the situation or client.

The tactile interpreter must strive to transmit the visual information as well as auditory input. The interpreter must first identify oneself, then tell the Deaf-Blind person who else is in the room. It is also important to identify who is talking each time the speaker changes. Facial expression and other visual or auditory nonverbal information should also be interpreted. Perhaps the Deaf-Blind client prefers the interpreter to express the nonverbal input, for example signing "SHE'S LAUGHING," or the Deaf-Blind person and the interpreter might devise a set of cues that indicate responses or facial, body and vocal expression. Manner of signing can also indicate some of the nonverbal portions of the utterance; e.g., sharp signing might show a speaker's crisp speaking style. Such communicative devices usually need to be agreed upon so that the client and interpreter are in sync with one another.

Timing is sometimes different in tactile interpreting, because it is seldom easy to interrupt and/or comment along the way. For example, often during an ordinary spoken conversation the listener will vocalize here and there, as a form of encouragement, things like "uhhuh," "really?" and other words, sounds or phrases. A signer in an ordinary signed conversation might sign "YES" or nod vigorously. This information is not easily accessible to a Deaf-Blind individual; so it might be wise for the Deaf-Blind person and the interpreter to work out a set of prearranged signals that can be used to respond to the speaker or to convey responses from listeners without interrupting.

Interpreting in situations involving Deaf-Blind individuals requires a degree of sensitivity and judgment that is possibly even greater than that required in general Sign Language interpreting.

Interpreting for D/deaf People with Minimal Language Competency

There are some people who, because of inadequate education, lack of exposure to society or language, or many other reasons, are not competent in any language. This means that they use neither English nor ASL, nor any other language fluently. These people have been labeled in a number of accurate and inaccurate ways. It is probably best to use the least judgmental terms possible, such as minimal language competency (MLC). There is no necessary correlation between intelligence and the communication skills of these people. Some highly intelligent people have never been given a chance to demonstrate their intelligence through language. There are, however, others who do not have the mental capacity necessary for the sophisticated use of language. One cannot always tell level of intelligence upon meeting a person with minimal language competency and therefore should not judge.

Often Deaf Interpreters work in teams with hearing interpreters to provide more effective interpretation in such settings as well as in many other settings, of course. The hearing interpreter passes information from spoken English on to the Deaf interpreter. The Deaf interpreter interprets to the MLC D/deaf person and when the MLC D/deaf person gestures, the Deaf interpreter signs the discourse in ASL or Signed English for the hearing interpreter to then interpret into spoken English. The Certified Deaf Interpreter (CDI) can often make a connection based on not only linguistic and cultural sophistication, but also based on their shared situation of D/deaf people. The client will often respond more quickly and efficiently with a Deaf interpreter, therefore saving time and money in the long run.

While interpreting in situations with D/deaf individuals having minimal language competency, there are many things that might allow the interpreter to communicate more effectively with the individual. It is important to clearly identify who is talking and to whom. It is also important to establish the role of the interpreter, because many people may have never experienced a situation involving an interpreter in the past. Some may have never even seen or heard of one.

It may be helpful to know that an interpreter can use any and all props in the room and rely on pointing whenever possible, as this is one of the clearest ways to refer to an object or person. Pictures can be very helpful. In fact some interpreters carry a picture book that shows a variety of concepts for quick and easy reference while interpreting. Often we can use rudimentary signs, such as "home signs", as well as ordinary gestures that are used and understood by signers and non-signers alike. Finally, something similar to pantomime can be heavily incorporated into the interpretation for a graphic demonstration of the concept.

Where minimal language competency is involved, the interpreter should remember to constantly check for understanding at each completed thought before moving on. This also means checking the vocabulary used to be sure it is understood. A good policy is to rely on the vocabulary used by the D/deaf client. Often areas that are familiar to the D/deaf client may differ from those that are familiar to the interpreter.

Usually fingerspelling should be avoided because English may not be known by the D/deaf client involved; however, any fingerspelled words introduced by the D/deaf client certainly can be used. Without knowing English it is possible the client will know some English words, especially words they have seen often, such as STOP or the name of a building, institution, city or person. However, the client may not understand script or even fingerspelling, so a printed word may occasionally help. The D/deaf client's facial expression can be watched as an indication of what is comfortable or understandable.

There is some temptation to treat D/deaf adults with minimal language competency like children because their language may seem childlike. We must treat them as adults and always give them the respect every adult deserves.

In reading information from a person with minimal language competency it is useful to keep in mind that not all nods of the head represent a "yes." Sometimes such a nod means, "yes, I understand"; other times a nod means "I'm being polite" or "I am listening/paying attention." Thus, it is important that the interpreter not vocalize a "yes" for a nod.

It is often helpful to first establish a baseline fact and ask questions based on that fact, such as "You live here now"; then "Where did you live last year?"

Time reference and time order should be carefully handled. We need to maintain consistency in tense and keep thoughts in time sequence as much as possible. It is usually helpful to keep tense as simple as possible and that means not switching tense, keeping time ordered events in their proper sequence, and clearly indicating any change in tense.

Facial and body expression of the interpreter are very important factors in minimal language competency interpreting. We must be concerned with how we affect the "interpreting climate" and try to create a comfortable environment for communication. While we must not try to change the atmosphere of the event, we should be sure we are not adding tension to it. Our faces and body language will be important in this respect.

Also facial expression and body language will be important in conveying the vocal expression of the speaker and in establishing the atmosphere intended by the speaker. We may find it difficult to display the proper expression if we show that we are working hard or are confused or frustrated. Once again it is important to control the nonverbal information sent.

Repetition and redundancy can be very helpful. Use repetition for clarity and to reiterate points that have already been discussed. Repeat vocabulary and phrases in new contexts. Repetition can be essential in questions, negatives, emphasis and to underscore key ideas.

Certainly interpreting in the minimal language competency setting has unusual challenges, and interpreting behavior must be modified to fit the need. Interpreting is not always simultaneous; in fact, it is often consecutive. Although the interpreter neither adds nor deletes anything from either client's information, the form of the interpretation is generally lengthy and very differently structured.

Interpreting in special situations is a topic which could continue indefinitely. Outlined here have been some of the more common situations in which an interpreter might serve. Certainly the ethics of interpreting remain the same, but certain modifications are necessary in the actual format. It will be important to have a bit of background information and to work on the specific skills required for such situations.

Thought Questions

1. What equipment can be used when interpreting for a D/deaf person who prefers to speak on the telephone?

2. Why should a Sign Language interpreter know about oral transmission?

3. List the communication methods used for interpreting where Deaf-Blind individuals are involved. Briefly describe these methods.

4. Why do Deaf-Blind clients sometimes prefer a combination of methods? How can this be beneficial to the interpreter as well?

5. List some bits of visual information the interpreter might need to transmit tactilely to a Deaf-Blind client.

6. Define minimal language competency.

7. List ten techniques that can be employed while interpreting for a D/deaf person with minimal language competency.

---

[1]An interpreter who is interested in oral transmission can contact the Alexander Graham Bell Association, Oral Deaf Adults Society or Registry of Interpreters for the Deaf for more information.

[2]Smith, Teresa. Guidelines: Practical Tips for Working and Socializing with Deaf-Blind Persons, Revised Edition. Burtonsville, MD: Linstok Press, 2000.

Chapter 9

Certification and the Registry of Interpreters for the Deaf

As the profession of Sign Language interpreting grew, interpreters realized the need for an organization that would represent them nationwide. As a result of this recognized need, a workshop was held in 1964, in Muncie, Indiana, at Ball State Teachers College, where the Registry of Interpreters for the Deaf (RID) had its official start. At this meeting some of the first guidelines were discussed and the term "professional" was applied to Sign Language interpreters. Until this time most interpreters were people who happened to know Sign Language and were willing to interpret. Often this was voluntary, and there were no interpreters whose major professional identification was with the task of interpreting, per se. Typically they were teachers of the D/deaf , children of D/deaf parents, parents of a D/deaf child, or religious workers who knew Sign Language and therefore were called upon to help when a communication need arose. There was no guarantee of excellence or skill. Although many were highly skilled, there were also many who either lacked sophisticated skills or were unaware of ethical behavior in an interpreting situation.

Let me stress that their main function was typically something other than communication. Often counselors, for example, were called upon to interpret for their clients as well as to counsel them. As the need for interpreters grew and the requirements became more highly standardized, interpreters became concerned with the development of an organization that would nurture the growth of this young profession.

The concerned interpreters and other professionals who formed the Registry of Interpreters for the Deaf set about the task of determining the professional interpreter's role and functions, as well as establishing the guidelines within which the Sign Language interpreter should operate. They possibly foresaw the advent of a professional interpreter whose primary function would be serving as a communication link, rather than that function being secondary to some other responsibility. Those pioneers have set the stage for our profession's growth.

Possibly the most significant step the RID has taken since its inception has been that of establishing evaluation procedures for certification of interpreters. Certification is an essential factor in any profession, as the general public cannot be responsible for knowing what constitutes skill in any area that takes a great deal of training and/or knowledge. For example, few patients are prepared to determine the medical competency of their doctors and nurses, nor can clients judge the skills necessary to be a qualified audiologist. Likewise our clients cannot always know if we are truly competent.

Until recently in some areas, and still the case in other areas, an interpreter was anyone who wanted to could be called an interpreter. Recognizing this weakness, the National Registry of Interpreters for the Deaf decided to establish a certification process. Materials were developed and an evaluation process and system was put forward. That system has been scrutinized and overhauled a number of times, producing a more reliable and valid test. Individuals can be tested at many sites and opportunities occur regularly to be evaluated. It should be mentioned here that the National Association of the Deaf took on the formidable task of developing another test for interpreters to be certified. Both RID and NAD have committed significant resources and effort toward the standardization and certification of interpreters. NAD and RID are working in concert to create a new joint certification procedure which will replace all former certification titles and systems when it is complete.

It should be stressed that certification, though a high honor, is merely the stamp of approval of basic skills. It indicates the basic ability to serve in the capacity of a Sign Language interpreter. There is no guarantee that the interpreter who receives certification can adequately serve in every situation encountered, but certification implies that the interpreter can serve in almost any situation. Certification is like getting a driver's license. Just as the driver's license gives the driver the right to drive on our streets and certifies basic competency behind the wheel, so RID certification establishes the basic competency of the Sign Language interpreter to interpret in most situations. It does not distinguish between various levels of interpreters, just as a driver's license does not qualify anyone for the "Indy 500." However, anyone who drives in the Indy 500 does first need to have a driver's license.

The purpose of the evaluation is to attempt a fair examination of the skills, knowledge and professionalism of the interpreter candidate. An interpreter can presently be evaluated and certified for generalist skills and specialized areas of interpreting through the RID and can be certified for levels through NAD. Testing procedures have been developed for both hearing and Deaf candidates. A generalist certificate is required to move on to a specialist certificate such as the SC:L (Specialist Certificate: Legal).

INTERPRETER TAKING RID EVALUATION

The process of evaluation begins with a warmup session for the candidate. The individual to be evaluated goes through a warmup session to get accustomed to working with the kinds of materials that will be used during the evaluation.

There are workshops and courses created specifically to assist candidates to prepare for evaluation for certification. Information cannot be shared as to the content of the tests, but training can assist potential candidates to become more comfortable with the process itself and perhaps the equipment and similar materials as well.

Evaluation is an important step in the professionalism of our field. It is hoped that all of us will make certification one of our goals and that we continue to strive to improve even after reaching that goal. Certification is a valuable tool for people both within and outside of our profession.

Thought Questions

1. Where were interpreters found before the Ball State Teachers college convention?

2. What major change has occurred since the introduction of the RID to the function of an interpreter?

3. Why do we need a Registry of Interpreters for the Deaf ?

4. What are some of the values of certification of interpreters?

5. What does certification indicate in terms of skill?

6. Write out three possible questions relating to the ethics of interpreting that could be asked in an evaluation for certification.

7. What other aspects of the interpreter are evaluated during the interview portion of the evaluation besides ethics?

8. What might be a useful way to prepare for certification evaluation?

Registry of Interpreters for the Deaf Code of Ethics

The Registry of Interpreters for the Deaf, Inc., has set forth the following principles of ethical behavior to protect and guide interpreters and transliterators and hearing and deaf consumers. Underlying these principles is the desire to insure for all the right to communicate.

This Code of Ethics applies to all members of the Registry of Interpreters for the Deaf, Inc., and to all certified non-members.

* Interpreters/transliterators shall keep all assignment-related information strictly confidential.

* Interpreters/transliterators shall render the message faithfully, always conveying the content and spirit of the speaker using language most readily understood by the person(s) whom they serve.

* Interpreters/transliterators shall not counsel, advise or interject personal opinions.

* Interpreters/transliterators shall accept assignments using discretion with regard to skill, setting, and the consumers involved.

* Interpreters/transliterators shall request compensation for services in a professional and judicious manner.

* Interpreters/transliterators shall function in a manner appropriate to the situation.

* Interpreters/transliterators shall strive to further knowledge and skills through participation in workshops, professional meetings, interaction with professional colleagues, and reading of current literature in the field.

* Interpreters/transliterators, by virtue of membership or certification by the RID, Inc., shall strive to maintain high professional standards in compliance with the Code of Ethics.

Certification

As research and practice lead us to new discoveries and understanding regarding the assessment of interpretation skills, knowledge and attitudes, certification practices shall further change to reflect those refinements.

Registry of Interpreters for the Deaf (RID) Certificates

The certificates described below are an indication that the interpreter or transliterator was assessed by a group of professional peers according to a nationally recognized standard of minimum competence. The individual's performance was deemed to meet or exceed this national standard.

RID Certificates are recognized as valid certificates provided the interpreter/transliterator meets all requirements of membership including participation in the Certification Maintenance Program. All interpreters and transliterators are required to adhere to the RID Code of Ethics governing ethical behavior within the profession. Violations of the Code of Ethics could result in a complaint filed against the interpreter/transliterator through the RID Ethical Practices System.

The RID National Testing System (NTS) strives to maintain

adherence to nationally recognized testing industry standards of validity, reliability and equity. As a result, an independent psychometrician (test development expert) is retained by RID and oversees test development and revision processes. RID maintains affiliation with the National Organization for Competency Assurance (NOCA), the entity that sets national criteria for validity, reliability and fairness in testing and credentialing.

CI (Certificate of Interpretation)

Holders of this certificate are recognized as fully certified in Interpretation and have demonstrated the ability to interpret between American Sign Language (ASL) and spoken English in both sign-to-spoken and spoken-to-sign. The interpreter's ability to transliterate is not considered in this certification.

CT (Certificate of Transliteration)

Holders of this certificate are recognized as fully certified in Transliteration and have demonstrated the ability to transliterate between English-based Sign Language and spoken English in both sign-to-spoken and spoken-to-sign. The transliterator's ability to interpret is not considered in this certification.

CI and CT (Certificate of Interpretation and Certificate of Transliteration)

Holders of both full certificates (as listed above) have demonstrated competence in both interpretation and transliteration and have the same flexibility of job acceptance as holders of the CSC listed below.

CLIP-R (Conditional Legal Interpreting Permit-Relay)

Holders of this conditional permit have completed an RID recognized training program designed for interpreters and transliterators who work in legal settings and who are also Deaf or hard-of-hearing. Generalist certification for interpreters/transliterators who are Deaf or hard-of-hearing (RSC or CDI-P) is required prior to enrollment in the training program. This permit is valid until one year after the Specialist Certificate: Legal written and performance test for Deaf interpreters is available nationally. CLIP-R holders must take and pass the new legal certification examination in order to maintain certification in the specialized area of interpreting in legal settings.

CDI-P (Certified Deaf Interpreter-Provisional)

Holders of this provisional certification are interpreters who are Deaf or hard-of-hearing and who have demonstrated a minimum of one year experience working as an interpreter, completion of at least 8 hours of training on the RID Code of Ethics, and 8 hours of training in general interpretation as it relates to the interpreter who is Deaf or hard-of-hearing. Provisional certification is valid until one year after the Certified Deaf Interpreter written and performance test is available nationally. Provisional certificate holders must take and pass the CDI examination in order to remain certified as a Deaf interpreter.

CDI (Certified Deaf Interpreter)

Holders of this certification are interpreters who are Deaf or hard-of-hearing and who have demonstrated a minimum of one year experience working as an interpreter, completion of at least 8 hours of training on the RID Code of Ethics, and 8 hours of training in general interpretation as it relates to the interpreter who is Deaf or hard-of-hearing. Holders of this certificate are recommended for a broad range of assignments where an interpreter who is Deaf or hard-of-hearing would be beneficial. This test is being revised and is not currently available.

SC:L (Specialist Certificate: Legal)

Holders of this specialist certificate have demonstrated specialized knowledge of legal settings and greater familiarity with language used in the legal system. Generalist certification and documented training and experience is required prior to sitting for this exam.

OTC (Oral Transliteration Certificate)

Holders of this generalist certificate have demonstrated ability to transliterate a spoken message from a person who hears to a person who is deaf or hard-of-hearing and the ability to understand and repeat the message and intent of the speech and mouth movements of the person who is deaf or hard-of-hearing.

National Association of the Deaf Certificates

The NAD Interpreter Assessment and Certification Program is housed at the NAD headquarters in Silver Spring, Maryland, and is operated by qualified state affiliates under cooperative agreement with the NAD.

Candidates desiring to achieve certification through the NAD program must first contact the local state affiliate for a pre-screening application. After satisfying the pre-screening requirements, the candidate will be scheduled for the assessment procedure.

After a brief warm-up period, the one hour assessment will begin. It includes a 15 to 20 minute interview segment focusing on knowledge and ethics of interpreting. The performance segment is approximately 45 minutes in length. An assessment videotape is utilized consisting of six typical interpreting situations from simple English translations to more complex ASL interpreting assessments. Candidates are required to interpret the segments using the appropriate sign system.

Evaluation is performed by a panel of five assessors selected for their knowledge and involvement in the field of interpreting, English and ASL proficiency, and interpreter skill expectations. A sixth member serves as the team interpreter and does not have scoring rights. A seventh member serves as a back-up. The panel consists of three deaf and two hearing raters.

There are five assessment levels –

Level I (Novice I)

Level II (Novice II)

Level III (Generalist)

Level IV (Advanced)

Level V (Master)

Only candidates who achieve Level III – V are certified as interpreters.

Resource Bibliography

ASL Across America Videotape. Burtonsville, MD: Sign Media, Inc., 1992.

ASL Numbers Videotape. Burtonsville, MD: Sign Media, Inc., 1989.

Baker, Charlotte and Padden, Carol. American Sign Language: A Look at its History, Structure, and Community. Silver Spring, MD, TJ Publishers, 1978.

Bienvenu, Colonomos. Intro to Deaf Culture – videos and workbooks. Burtonsville, MD: Sign Media, Inc., 1991.

Bienvenu, MJ, & Colonomos, B. Relay Interpreting in the '90s. In L. Swabey (Ed.), *Proceedings of the Eighth National Convention of the Conference of Interpreter Trainers* (pp. 69-80). Conference of Interpreter Trainers, 1990.

Bornstein, Harry, Saulnier, Karen, and Hamilton, Lillian, editors. Comprehensive Signed English Dictionary. Washington, DC: Gallaudet University Press, 1983.

Bowen-Bailey, D. The challenges of educational interpreting. Views, 13(3), 16-17, 1996.

Collins, S.D. Deaf-Blind Interpreting: The structure of ASL and the interpreting process. In E.A. Winston (Ed.) *Gallaudet University communication forum 1993 (pp.20-36).* Washington, DC: Gallaudet University School of Communication, 1993.

Costello, E. <u>Random House Webster's American Sign Language Medical Dictionary.</u> New York: Random House, 2000.

Costello, E. <u>Religious Signing: A Comprehensive Guide for all Faiths.</u> New York: Bantam Books, 1986.

De Jongh, E.M. <u>Introduction to court interpreting: Theory and practice.</u> Lanham, MD: University Press of America, 1993.

<u>Deaf-Blind Communication and Community Videotape Set.</u> Burtonsville, MD: Sign Media, Inc., 1992.

Edwards, A.B. <u>The Practice of Court Interpreting.</u> Philadelphia: John Benjamins, 1995.

<u>Face of ASL Videotape Series.</u> Burtonsville, MD: Sign Media, Inc., 1991.

Fant , L., <u>The American Sign Language Phrase Book.</u> Chicago, Illinois: Contemporary Books, 1994.

Fant, L. *Silver threads: A personal look at the first twenty-five years of the Registry of Interpreters for the D/deaf.* Silver Spring, MD: Rid Publications, 1990.

<u>Fingerspelling Practice Videotape Series.</u> Burtonsville, MD: Sign Media, Inc., 1991.

Fischer, T. <u>Establishing a Freelance Interpretation Business.</u> Hillsboro, Oregon: Butte Publications, 1998.

Fisher, T. Team interpreting: The "team" approach. Journal of Interpreting, 6(1), 167-174, 1993.

FitzPatrick, T. *Deaf interpreters and hearing interpreters as members of an interesting team.* Unpublished manuscript, Gallaudet University, Dept. of Linguistics and Interpreting, Washington, DC, 1993.

Fleetwood, E., Metzger, M. Cued speech transliteration: Theory and Application. Silver Spring, MD: Calliope Press, 1990.

Frishberg, N. Interpreting: An Introduction. Silver Spring, MD: Registry of Interpreters for the Deaf, 1990.

Gebron, J. Sign the Speech: An Introduction to Theatrical Interpreting. Hillsboro, Oregon: Butte Publications, 2000.

Gile, D. Basic Concepts and Models for Interpreter and Translator Training. Philadelphia: John Benjamins, 1995.

Guillory, LaVera M. Expressive and Receptive Fingerspelling for Hearing Adults. Baton Rouge, LA: Claitor's Publishing Division, 1966.

Gustason, Gerilee and Zawolkow, Esther. Signing Exact English. Alameda, CA: Modern Signs Press.

Hayes, P.L. Educational interpreters for deaf students: Their responsibilities, problems and concerns. *Journal of Interpretation,* 5(1), 5-23, 1992.

Hoza, J. Doing the right thing: Interpreter roles and ethics within a bilingual/bicultural model. In L. Swabey (Ed.), *The challenge of the 90's; New standards in interpreter education. Proceedings of the Eighth National Convention of the Conference of Interpreter Trainers* (pp. 101-117). Conference of Interpreter Trainers, 1990.

Humphries, Padden, O'Rourke. A Basic Course in American Sign Language. Silver Spring, MD: TJ Publishers, 1994.

Interpreter Practice Materials Videotape Series. Burtonsville, MD: Sign Media, Inc., 1996.

Interpreters on Interpreting Videotape Series. Burtonsville, MD: Sign Media, Inc., 1989.

Interpreting in the American Legal System Videotape Series and Workbook. Burtonsville, MD: Sign Media, Inc., 1993.

Interpreting the Miranda Warnings Videotape. Burtonsville, MD: Sign Media, Inc., 1992.

Introduction to Deaf Community Videotape. Burtonsville, MD: Sign Media, Inc., 1992

James, R. RID Certification Maintenance Program. In E.A. Winston (Ed.), *Mapping our course: A collaborative venture, Proceedings of the Tenth National Convention of the Conference of Interpreter Trainers* (pp.237-244). Conference of Interpreter Trainers, 1995.

Jamison, S. Signs for Computing Terminology. Silver Spring, MD: National Association of the D/deaf, 1983.

Lane, Hoffmeister, Bahan. A Journey into the Deaf World. San Diego, CA: Dawn Sign Press, 1996.

Langdon, H.W., & Others. *The interpreter translator process in the educational setting: A resource manual.* (ERIC Document Reproduction Service No. ED 383 155), 1994.

Lentz, Mikos, Smith. Signing Naturally Series. San Diego, CA: Dawn Sign Press, 1988.

Mattice, S.L. Language policies and the role of the educational interpreter. Unpublished manuscript, Gallaudet University, Department of Linguistics and Interpreting, Washington, DC, 1994.

McIntire, M.L., & Sanderson, G.R. Bye-bye!: Questions of empowerment and role. In A confluence of diverse relationships: Proceedings of the Thirteenth National Convention of Registry of Interpreters for the Deaf. (pp. 94-118). Silver Spring, MD: Registry of Interpreters for the Deaf, 1993.

Metzger, M. Sign Language Interpreting: Deconstructing the Myth of Neutrality. Washington, DC: Gallaudet University Press, 1999.

Moxham, T. How to Use a Sign Language Interpreter. Hillsboro, OR: Butte Publications, 1996.

Nettles, C. NAD/RID Task Force votes to develop joint testing instrument. Views, 13(7), 1, 23-24, 1996.

Overuse Syndrome Video. Burtonsville, MD: Sign Media, Inc., 1992.

Padden, C., Humphries, T. Deaf in American, Voices from a Culture. Cambridge, MA: Harvard University Press, 1988.

Shaw, R. A conversation: Written feedback notes while team interpreting. In E.A. Winston (Ed.), *Mapping our course: A collaborative venture. Proceedings of the Tenth National Convention of the Conference of Interpreter Trainers* (pp. 245-275). Conference of Interpreter Trainers, 1995.

Shaw, R. Preparing yourself to be an effective legal interpreter. Views, 13(7), 1, 24-25, 1996.

Smith Theresa. Guidelines for Working and Socializing with Deaf-Blind People: Revised Edition. Burtonsville, MD: Linstok Press, 2000.

Stokoe, William C.; Croneberg, Carl G.; Casterline, Dorothy C. A Dictionary of American Sign Language on Linguistic Principles. Burtonsville, MD: Linstok Press, 1976.

Technical Signs Project, Technical Signs Series. Rochester: NY: National Technical Institute for the Deaf, 1975.

Using a Sign Language Interpreter Videotape. Burtonsville, MD: Sign Media, Inc., 1993.

Wilcox, Sherman, editor. American Deaf Culture: An Anthology. Burtonsville, MD: Linstok Press, 1989

Woodward, James. <u>Signs of Drug Use</u>. Silver Spring, MD: TJ
    Publishers, 1980

Woodward, James. <u>Signs of Sexual Behavior</u>. Silver Spring,
    MD: TJ Publishers, 1979.

<u>Working with a Sign Language Interpreter Videotape</u>.
    Burtonsville, MD: Sign Media, Inc., 1993.

About the Author

Sharon Neumann Solow works as an interpreter, interpreter coordinator, performer, lecturer and consultant. Her career has taken her around the United States, and to Canada, Mexico, Europe, Scandinavia, New Zealand and Australia. She is the author of two books, <u>Sign Language Interpreting: A Basic Resource Book</u> and <u>Say It With Sign</u> (which she is presently revising) along with a number of professional articles and handbooks. Her television appearances include talk shows, variety shows and documentaries and she co-stars with her husband, Larry Solow, on the Emmy award-nominated NBC Knowledge series, "Say It With Sign" which still airs throughout the United States. As the female lead in "The Electric Sign Company", she and Gary Sanderson have delighted audiences throughout America. She is a working interpreter, mostly in legal and conference settings, with a long history of classroom interpreting and educational interpreter training and administration. In court, she specializes in working with D/deaf people with minimal language skills. Her travels and some of her conference work have involved the use of international gesture (a gestural, pantomimic form of communication across language barriers) interpreting. Sharon is an active member of the RID (Registry of Interpreters for the Deaf) and CIT (Conference of Interpreter Trainers), holding the Specialist Certificate: Legal as well as the NAD (National

Association of the Deaf) SIGN (Sign Language Instructor Guidance Network) Comprehensive Permanent Certificate. The 1987 recipient of the national Virginia Hughes Award for outstanding contributions to the field of Sign Language interpreting, Sharon has lived on the Monterey Peninsula since 1984. She and her husband have two wonderful children, Megan and Jered.